Amazing Facts in World History

By
DON BLATTNER

COPYRIGHT © 2003 Mark Twain Media, Inc.

ISBN 1-58037-238-4

Printing No. CD-1584

Mark Twain Media, Inc., Publishers
Distributed by Carson-Dellosa Publishing Company, Inc.

Table of Contents

Introduction

There are two problems when studying world history. First, some of the most interesting, bizarre, and tantalizing stories are ignored. These are the stories and facts that students would really enjoy, but they are usually considered to be unimportant. Here are a few examples.

- In Mesopotamia: Each year there would be a public celebration where the king would have his ears pulled, and he would be slapped in the face until he cried.
- Ancient Egypt: When a pet cat died, the family would shave their eyebrows. Egyptians hunted with boomerangs and wore kilts. When King Tut died, his widow married her grandfather. In order to cure a sick baby, an Egyptian mother would sometimes eat a mouse.
- Ancient Rome: When Romans feasted, they wouldn't sit at a table; they would recline three to a couch. When a guest was enjoying a feast at a banquet, he would sometimes go to the bathroom at the table, so he wouldn't have to leave. He might also vomit so that he could continue eating. In Roman bathhouses, there were snack bars, gift shops, and libraries. Men wore loin cloths to bathhouses, while some of the women wore bikinis.
- Mongols: One of the main jobs of a Mongol woman was to slit throats. Mongols tenderized their dried meat by putting it under their saddles. When Mongols were away from their homes and had no food, they would drink their horses' milk and blood.
- Vikings: Vikings believed that the first humans came from the sweat of a giant's armpit.
- Ancient Greece: Sporting events were held at funerals. Athletes in the original Olympics competed naked. The Greeks invented the flame thrower, yo-yos, spinning tops, and marionettes.
- Medieval Times: Almost everyone drank beer for breakfast.
- Inquisition: A person could be charged with heresy for not eating pork or not drinking alcoholic beverages. Prisoners found guilty of heresy were forced to march in a procession and wear a dunce's cap. It was possible for someone to be brought to trial and to have his property confiscated, even though he was dead.
- The Age of Reason: If a person committed suicide in France, the corpse was hanged.
- World War I: A pigeon was awarded the Distinguished Service Cross for saving a battalion.
- Sports: The oldest person to complete a marathon was 98 years old. The oldest person to win a medal in the Olympics was 72.

The second problem in studying world history is that many of the "facts" we have learned in school or which have been passed down from past generations are either not true, or cannot be documented. Some of them may have began as a story that someone told a grandchild, and the grandchild passed it along, and eventually, it was published and became part of folklore. In other cases, events have been recorded by individuals who either hated or liked certain historical figures and purposely lied about what actually happened. Here are some examples:

- Nero did **not** fiddle or play while Rome burned. He was 50 miles away.
- Cleopatra was **not** beautiful by today's idea of beauty, and she wasn't even an Egyptian.
- The pyramids were built by hired workers, not slaves.
- The iceberg that sank the Titanic did not rip a hole in the hull.

Introduction (cont.)

This book is designed as a series of quizzes that includes these as well as many other amazing facts of world history. It doesn't deal with all of the important issues that students learn in school. Instead, by revealing little-known facts, it gives a personal, intimate view of the people and events that have shaped the world.

This book is especially valuable as a pre-learning activity. Prior to studying a unit, one of the tests from this book should pique a student's interest, arouse his or her curiosity, and give a different perspective to what he or she is about to learn. It will be a springboard for discussion.

Just as important as the facts and answers are the explanations after each quiz. The explanation of the correct answer gives elaborate details concerning these unusual historical facts. The answers and explanations are printed directly after the questions, so they can be duplicated and given to the students for further study.

In addition to the quizzes, there are puzzles and logic problems dealing with world history. Some are very easy, while others may be quite challenging. Also, there is a section called "Mysteries From History." These are actual historical mysteries that students are invited to solve. They can solve the mystery by themselves, in groups, or the teacher may present the mystery as a twenty-question type of activity. In this case, the teacher would read the mystery to the class, and the students would try to solve it by asking the teacher questions. The teacher can only answer "yes" or "no" to the questions.

Here's one other suggestion. The class may choose to start its own list of strange and unusual facts of history discovered while doing their own research. The list could then be printed and distributed for the students at the end of the year.

Name: _____   Date: _____

Mesopotamia and Sumer

Mesopotamia is the area between the Tigris and Euphrates Rivers. It is one of the places where civilization first began. It is where humans settled, farmed, built cities, developed metal technology, invented writing, and kept records. The land we once called Mesopotamia is now known as Iraq, northern Syria, and southern Turkey. Sumer was a region in southern Mesopotamia.

Circle the letter of the answer you believe correctly completes each statement.

1. On March the 21st of each year, there would be a public celebration where the Mesopotamian king would be:
   A. Praised by the people.
   B. Given gold to make the crops grow.
   C. Required to dress like a donkey.
   D. Slapped until he cried.

2. Mesopotamians learning to be scribes were taught by people they called:
   A. Wise one.
   B. Big brother.
   C. Teacher.
   D. Master.

3. The school's principal was called:
   A. Lord.
   B. School father.
   C. Honorable man.
   D. Wise leader.

4. The Mesopotamians wrote the first:
   A. Farmer's almanac.
   B. Geography book.
   C. Book on beauty aids.
   D. Medical text.

5. Some Mesopotamian homes had:
   A. Flush toilets.
   B. Whirlpool baths.
   C. Swimming pools.
   D. Overhead fans.

6. Mesopotamians believed that a person could become ill or unlucky by breaking certain rules or committing sins. One such rule was, on the first day of the month, "thou shall not:
   A. look at your wife."
   B. eat garlic, or a scorpion will sting you."
   C. work, or your crops will fail."
   D. conduct business, or you will be beaten."

7. Instead of praying to gods for their souls, Mesopotamians:
   A. Had slaves pray for them.
   B. Hired people to pray for them.
   C. Had statues pray for them.
   D. Bought the souls of others.

8. When someone in a prominent family died, they were usually buried:
   A. In a temple.
   B. Under the floor of his or her house.
   C. In a castle.
   D. In the royal sepulcher.

Name: _____   Date: _____

Mesopotamia and Sumer (cont.)

9. Which of the following did the Mesopotamians **not** use to foretell the future?
    A. Studying the stars   B. Studying the flight of birds
    C. Studying the intestines of animals   D. Studying the shells of turtles

10. Scribes kept records and wrote letters and reports on clay tablets. Important legal documents were often put in an envelope and given to Temple Scribes to keep. The envelopes were made of:
    A. Papyrus.   B. Papier-mâché.
    C. Clay.   D. Reeds.

11. After a Sumerian died, the worse thing that could happen was for him:
    A. To be buried in a foreign land.   B. To be cremated.
    C. Not to be buried by sundown.   D. Not to be buried.

12. In the country, most houses:
    A. Did not have chapels.   B. Did not have a courtyard.
    C. Did not have doors.   D. Were made of wood.

13. When a visitor arrived at a home:
    A. A slave washed his feet.   B. He was immediately given a huge meal.
    C. He was given wine and dates.   D. He was expected to pay his host.

14. The favorite Sumerian drink was:
    A. Goat's milk.   B. Beer.
    C. Wine.   D. Water.

15. In ancient Sumer, Nanna was the name for:
    A. Nursemaid.   B. Grandmother.
    C. The Moon god.   D. Banana.

16. Which of the following was the head of a Sumerian household forbidden to do?
    A. Take property from his slave   B. Divorce his wife
    C. Sell his wife into slavery   D. Sell his children into slavery

17. In order to improve their appearance, Sumerians would:
    A. Wear cucumbers over their eyes.   B. Clean their faces with olive oil.
    C. Rub their faces with stones.   D. Wear tattoos.

18. During the growing season, the farmer would always pray to the Goddess of:
    A. The Harvest.   B. Sun and Rain.
    C. Earth and Wind.   D. Mice and Vermin.

Mesopotamia and Sumer Answers

1. **D. Slapped until he cried.** Mesopotamians had several important festivals during the year. Over a period of time, many of these festivals were merged into one New Year's celebration that lasted 11 days. This celebration happened during the spring equinox, which occurs about March 21st. There were ceremonies and sacrifices. On the fifth day, the king was humiliated by having a priest take his royal clothes away from him, pull his ears, and slap him in the face until he cried. The purpose of the ceremony was to remind everyone that the king was a mortal and that he, too, was a servant of the gods.

2. **B. Big brother.**

3. **B. School father.**

4. **A. Farmer's almanac.** Somewhere between 5000 and 4000 B.C., the first farmer's almanac was written by a Sumerian teacher. This farmer's book explained the annual flooding of the fields, how to plant crops, how to care for them, and how to harvest them. It also taught how to raise animals.

5. **A. Flush toilets.** Mesopotamian towns had clay pipes used for drainage.

6. **B. Eat garlic, or a scorpion will sting you."**

7. **C. Had statues pray for them.** Mesopotamians prayed to the gods and asked for long and prosperous lives. Ordinary people were not allowed to go inside the temples, and those who were wealthy did not have the time to spend praying; so some people would hire an artist to make a stone statue of a Sumerian praying. The statue was to pray for the person for whom the statue was made.

Enki, the Sumerian god of water

8. **B. Under the floor of his or her house.** Or they were sometimes buried near a family shrine often located behind the house. When a Sumerian king died, all the members of his household, which included the ladies of the court, guards, musicians, and soldiers, would take poison and be buried with him. They did this so they could serve the king in the afterlife.

9. **D. Studying the shells of turtles.** Mesopotamians felt that their lives were completely controlled by the gods. They tried many methods to determine the fate the gods had in mind for them. Mesopotamians believed that diviners could tell the future by studying the weather, the stars and the planets, the flight of birds, or the entrails of sacrificial animals. Mesopotamians also believed that if a person learned of the bad fate in store for them, they could change the future by performing certain rituals or by trying to fool fate. For example, if a fortuneteller said that a king was going to die, a substitute king would be crowned and allowed to rule for a certain length of time. Then the substitute would be killed and buried, so the prophesy could be fulfilled. Afterwards, the real king

Mesopotamia and Sumer Answers (cont.)

could be restored to his throne and live a long life. On one occasion, however, it did not work out as planned. A fortuneteller had predicted that the king was going to die, so the king had his gardener crowned as king. He planned to kill the gardener later and then be restored to the throne. However, while the gardener was king, the real king happened to die. So, the gardener ruled for the next 24 years.

10. **C. Clay.**
11. **D. Not to be buried.** If he were not buried, it was thought that he became an evil spirit and haunted his relatives.
12. **C. Did not have doors.** Wood was so valuable that those who owned anything made of wood considered it a valuable asset. Many houses did not have doors, and those with doors did not consider them as part of the property. If the house was sold, the door was sold separately or was taken by the seller to his new home. Most homes in ancient Sumeria included a small family tomb. Next to the tomb was a chapel.
13. **A. A slave washed his feet.**
14. **B. Beer.** The Mesopotamians produced 19 different types of beer.
15. **C. The Moon god.**
16. **A. Take property from his slave.** A father was the head of the household and master of the house. If his wife did not bear children, he was allowed to divorce her. It was even possible for him to sell his wife and children into slavery. Children were sometimes sold into slavery in order to pay the debts of the parents. Slaves in ancient Sumeria were treated better than slaves were in other civilizations. They were considered a valuable part of the community. While slavery was not a good life, slaves did enjoy some legal rights. They could borrow money, engage in business activities, and even buy their freedom. If a free man married a slave, their children would be considered free. Slave families were never separated, unless the members of the slave family gave their consent. If a male slave was sold, his wife and children were sold along with him. If a slave was not married, a master might buy him a female slave to marry. A slave could own property and was able to farm and to even own a house. His master could not take these things away from him. In the country, when a farmer sold a farm, the slaves were included in the sale. The slaves were considered property and part of the farm.
17. **C. Rub their faces with stones.** Sumerians wore very heavy makeup. Men and women alike used eyeliner and eyeshadow. They darkened their eyebrows and eyelashes. Some kings even wore false beards to make them look more distinguished. They often smoothed their faces with pumice stones. Pumice stones are a kind of a volcanic glass; it was lightweight and was used to smooth and polish. Sumerians also curled their hair and doused it with perfume. They took perfumed baths. They painted their faces with white lead and their lips and cheeks with red henna. Red henna was also applied to their fingernails and the palms of their hands.
18. **D. Mice and Vermin.** The purpose of a prayer was to prevent these animals from destroying the crops.

Name: _____ Date: _____

Egyptian Life

A civilization began in Egypt on the banks of the Nile River over 5,000 years ago. This civilization, along with Mesopotamia, India, and China, was one of the earliest and most important civilizations. Its form of writing, hieroglyphics; its art; and other features of its culture were adopted by other ancient kingdoms and civilizations. The ancient Egyptians' influence extended centuries after Egypt ceased to be a great civilization.

Circle the letter of the answer(s) you believe correctly completes each statement.

1. Which of the following were **not** traditional hunting weapons used by ancient Egyptians?
   A. Boomerangs
   B. Bows and arrows
   C. Traps
   D. Razors

2. In order to cure a sick baby, a mother would sometimes:
   A. Eat a mouse.
   B. Beat herself.
   C. Bathe the child in water from the Nile.
   D. Feed the child hippopotamus fat.

3. When Egyptians hunted crocodiles, they would:
   A. Catch them with baited hooks.
   B. Catch them with nets.
   C. Kill them as they slept.
   D. Throw them poisoned fish.

4. During harvest time, landowners would often hire:
   A. A rain dancer.
   B. Musicians.
   C. Wagons and carts.
   D. Priests.

5. The bread made by the Egyptians caused:
   A. Cancer.
   B. People to lose their teeth.
   C. Hallucinations.
   D. Blindness.

6. Upper Egypt was in the:
   A. North.
   B. South.
   C. East.
   D. West.

7. Which of the following were **not** used to move people and goods in ancient Egypt?
   A. Donkeys
   B. Horses
   C. Camels
   D. Sleds

8. Egyptian men would wear loincloths or:
   A. Short shorts.
   B. Dresses.
   C. Serapes.
   D. Kilts.

9. When an ancient Egyptian went to a banquet, the host might place a cone containing animal fat mixed with perfume:
   A. On the head of the guest.
   B. On the table.
   C. On his dinner plate.
   D. In the guest's hands.

Name: _____ Date: _____

Egyptian Life (cont.)

10. Eye paint was used by men as well as women. The purpose of the eye paint was not only to enhance the eyes and improve the appearance of the person wearing it, but it also:
    A. Kept away the flies.
    B. Kept them cool.
    C. Revealed their occupation.
    D. Showed if they were married or single.

11. Which of the following cosmetics did the Egyptians **not** have?
    A. Dandruff remover
    B. Lotions to cure baldness
    C. Hair dyes
    D. Anti-wrinkle creams

12. In most Egyptian homes, there was a small altar or shrine for worshiping the gods. One of the gods that protected women who were having babies and raising children was a:
    A. Beautiful woman.
    B. Pregnant hippopotamus.
    C. White cat.
    D. God named "Guy No Cologist."

13. Many professional musicians were:
    A. Aristocrats.
    B. Blind.
    C. Soldiers.
    D. Slaves.

14. Which of the following medical procedures or practices was **not** used by the ancient Egyptians?
    A. Cosmetic surgery
    B. Sterilizing surgical instruments
    C. Brain surgery
    D. Open-heart surgery

15. The Egyptians considered the temple as a place where:
    A. Baptisms took place.
    B. Worship services were held.
    C. The gods lived.
    D. All of the above.

16. When Egyptians went to the temple gates to pray, they sometimes propped a slab of stone against the wall. On the stone were:
    A. Written prayers.
    B. Recipes for soup.
    C. Pictures of the god.
    D. Pictures of ears.

17. At a location called _____, the Egyptians worshipped _____.
    A. Sunni-dee, the Sun god
    B. Thebes, the Nile
    C. Crocodilopolis, the crocodile god
    D. Memphis, King Presley

18. After the flood had receded and farmers were able to work their land, they would sow their seed and then:
    A. Bury a dead fish in the ground.
    B. Allow pigs to run over the field.
    C. Have a priest bless the land.
    D. Sacrifice a lamb.

19. Anyone who wore colored clothing in ancient Egypt was probably a:
    A. Foreigner.
    B. Nobleman.
    C. Priest.
    D. Politician.

Name: _____ Date: _____

Egyptian Life (cont.)

20. When Egyptian houses became old and began to fall apart, the bricks were often used:
    A. To build a new house.
    B. To build a shrine.
    C. To build a sidewalk.
    D. For fertilizer.

21. A person considered it an honor to kiss the king's foot, while others would:
    A. Kiss his ring.
    B. Kiss the ground in front of the king.
    C. Bow in his presence.
    D. Name their children after him.

22. In ancient Egypt, almost one-third of the days were:
    A. Holy days.
    B. Spent working for the king.
    C. Spent in prayer.
    D. Spent working on the pyramids.

23. Egyptians may have been the first society to compile a:
    A. Cookbook.
    B. Medical text.
    C. Dictionary.
    D. Camel train schedule.

24. Farmers needed to protect their crops from cattle, birds, and:
    A. Wild pigs.
    B. Shuttlecocks.
    C. The king's army.
    D. Hippopotami.

25. When a doctor was unable to heal the patient with traditional types of medicine, he might use magic because it was thought that some diseases were caused by dead spirits. If the doctor thought that a specific dead person was causing the illness, then the doctor might:
    A. Attack the dead person's tomb.
    B. Make an offering to the dead person.
    C. Pray to the dead person.
    D. Threaten a relative of the dead person.

26. An Egyptian soldier wore a:
    A. Coat of armor.
    B. Suit of heavy leather.
    C. Coat made from a young goat.
    D. Short skirt made of linen.

27. Slaves in ancient Egypt had many different names. Which of the following was **not** the name for a slave?
    A. Listeners
    B. Cupbears
    C. Know-nothings
    D. Followers

28. Workers in stone quarries would split rock by:
    A. Using iron chisels.
    B. Using fire and water.
    C. Dropping them from cliffs.
    D. Using a huge guillotine.

29. About 1500 B.C., Egyptian women:
    A. Dyed their hair.
    B. Braided their hair.
    C. Combed their hair over their eyes.
    D. Polished their heads.

Egyptian Life Answers

1. **D. Razors.** Ancient Egyptian hunters used bows and arrows, as well as spears and nets to catch wild animals. They would use traps for birds, turtles, and hares. Strangely enough, they would also hunt with a boomerang. The boomerang was introduced into Egypt from Nubia and central Africa.

2. **A. Eat a mouse.**

3. **A. Catch them with baited hooks.** They would bait a hook with pork and throw it out into the middle of a river. Then they would beat a live pig, and when the crocodile heard the pig squeal, it would think that a pig had fallen into the river and take the bait. The men would then haul the crocodile out of the water and slap mud into its eyes. Since the crocodile could not see, it could be killed very easily. They would also hunt crocodiles with spears.

4. **B. Musicians.** Musicians would play flutes in order to keep the peasants entertained while they harvested the grain.

5. **B. People to lose their teeth.** Grains were the most important crops of the ancient Egyptians. With the wheat they grew, they were able to make about forty different kinds of breads, cakes, and other pastries. One of their biggest challenges, however, was to grind the grain into flour. This was a task assigned to women, who would grind the grain using stones. The grinding was done outside, and small bits of stone, dirt, and other objects became mixed with the flour. Over time, these foreign objects in the bread would cause the Egyptians to wear away their teeth and cause infections and other dental problems.

6. **B. South.**

7. **C. Camels.** Donkeys were the beasts of burden in ancient Egypt. While the Egyptians had horses, they were very expensive and mainly used to pull chariots. Sleds, sometimes called sledges, had been used since prehistoric times. Camels, which are often thought of as the beasts of burden in the East, had not yet been domesticated at the time of the ancient Egyptians.

8. **D. Kilts.** In early Egypt, women wore simple, straight dresses while men wore kilts and loincloths. A man would work only in a loincloth or nothing. Children very often would not wear any clothing.

9. **A. On the head of the guest.** Ancient Egyptians were very concerned about their appearance. They used many different types of oils, cleansing creams, and perfumes to protect their skin, improve their appearance, and combat body odors. When an ancient Egyptian went to a banquet, the host might place a cone that contained animal fat mixed with perfume on the head of the guest. As the animal fat melted and ran down the face and the back of the guest, it not only cooled the guest, it made him smell better.

10. **A. Kept away the flies.** Lead ore was used as a mascara or to make eye makeup. Lipstick was made of iron oxides, and a blush was put on the cheeks. The eyebrows were plucked. Nails were painted; sometimes the palms of their hands and the soles of the feet were even painted.

11. **They had them all.** In addition, there were lotions to prevent hair loss. Of course that doesn't mean they all worked.

Egyptian Life Answers (cont.)

12. **B. Pregnant hippopotamus.**

13. **B. Blind.** While those of royal blood would often learn to play musical instruments and learn to sing, professional musicians were hired to play at parties and at festivals. Since music was not written down as it is today, becoming a musician was something a blind person could do and still earn a living.

14. **D. Open-heart surgery.** The ancient Egyptians had a fairly accurate knowledge of the human body and how the organs worked because of their practice of preparing mummies. There were aware, for example, that if one side of the brain was injured, it would affect the workings of the opposite side of the body. There is some evidence that ancient Egyptians even practiced a rudimentary type of brain surgery. They also used some types of sedatives so a patient would not be in pain during surgery. While we are not sure of the type of sedatives used, it could have been opium or alcohol. The Egyptians attached a lot of ritual to their surgery. They would purify the instruments and themselves by washing themselves and by putting the surgical instruments in a fire before the operation. While these were done for religious reasons, both of these practices probably help cut down infection following surgery.

    When a patient came to a doctor, the doctor would first examine him very carefully. He would touch the patient, smell the patient, and then look him over. Then he would ask the patient many questions about his illness or injury. If he thought that he could cure the patient, he would say, "An ailment I will treat." If the doctor was uncertain if he could cure the patient, he would say, "An ailment with which I will contend." Unfortunately, there were times when the doctor knew that he would be unable to cure the patient. When this occurred, he would say, "An ailment not to be treated." Doctors would take notes of their treatments, the medicines they used, and how well they worked. They would use these notes when they treated other patients in the future. Some of the medicines the Egyptian doctors used were found to be very sound herbal treatments and worked remarkably well. On the other hand, some of the medicines they made were bizarre and, in some cases, even disgusting. The ingredients of some medicines included beetles, dung, and mice.

15. **C. The gods lived.** When a person sees or hears the word, "temple," there is a tendency to compare it to a modern-day church, synagogue or mosque. However, an Egyptian temple was not a place to hold worship services. The Egyptians considered the temple as a place where a god or goddess lived when he or she was on earth. Ordinary Egyptians were usually not allowed inside the temples to see the statues of the gods and goddesses. If a citizen wanted to pray to a god, he or she would go to the temple gate. Each temple generally had a priest and sometimes deputy priests. There were also priestesses who sang hymns. Sometimes there were professional musicians, singers, and dancers. The staff often included cooks, butchers, bakers, and brewers, who prepared food to offer to the gods. There were maintenance men, cleaners, and slaves to maintain the temple.

16. **D. Pictures of ears.** The stone was considered an offering to the god, but it was also a plea for the god to listen to the man's prayers.

Egyptian Life Answers (cont.)

17. **C. Crocodilopolis, the crocodile god.** In ancient Egypt, every town had its own god. This god would not be known or worshiped by people living in other towns but only by the people living in this particular town. Egyptians worshipped snakes, cats, cows, and even crocodiles. There was a whole group of people who worshipped the crocodile god at a place called Crocodilopolis. At Crocodilopolis, there was a crocodile. The priests would bring him gifts of bread, meat, and wine as he was lying on the bank. They would secure him so that he could not hurt them. Then they would pry his mouth open and force the bread, meat, and wine down his mouth. The priests would then retreat, and the crocodile would run away.

18. **B. Allow pigs to run over the field.** The pigs would force the seed into the ground.

19. **A. Foreigner.** Egyptians generally wore white clothing in order to keep cool. The light color would reflect the sunlight, while dark clothing absorbed the heat. Since almost everyone wore white clothing in ancient Egypt, anyone who wore colored clothing was probably a foreigner.

20. **D. For fertilizer.** Egyptian houses were made from wood, mud, and reeds. The mud bricks were often made from the rich silt that was the result of the flooding each spring. Because this mud was rich in nutrients, Egyptian farmers would often dismantle old homes that were falling apart and use the mud bricks for fertilizer.

21. **B. Kiss the ground in front of the king.**

22. **A. Holy days.**

23. **B. Medical text.** Egyptians who became doctors learned from experienced doctors. They actually kept track of the patients they treated and how successful the medicine and treatments were. In this way, they could use their experiences to treat future patients. As their knowledge of medicine increased, their notes were compiled into a document that is now known as the Edwin Smith Papyrus. This document gives the treatment and care of 48 different injuries.

24. **D. Hippopotami.**

25. **A. Attack the dead person's tomb.** By attacking and destroying the tomb of the evil spirit causing the illness, it was thought that the spirit would be released.

26. **D. Short skirt made of linen.**

27. **C. Know-nothings.** Slaves were often named after the tasks they performed. They were sometimes called listeners, because they listened to and obeyed orders. They were also called followers or cupbears.

28. **B. Using fire and water.** The workers placed wedges of wood into the cracks and then doused the wood with water, making the wedges swell, thereby cracking the rock. Sometimes, they would set fires inside the cracks or rocks and then douse the fires with cold water. The sudden change in temperature of the rock from hot to cold would cause the rock to split.

29. **D. Polished their heads.** A shaved head was the fashion and considered beautiful. Egyptian women plucked every hair from their heads and polished their scalps. Priests in Egyptian temples also plucked every hair from their bodies, including their eyebrows and eyelashes.

Name: _____ Date: _____

The Egyptian Way of Death

Mummies are dead humans or animals that have been preserved. Mummies have been found in many different countries. In some cases, those burying the dead intentionally tried to preserve the bodies by mummifying them. In other cases, the environment has preserved the bodies. Frozen mummies have been found in Greenland, Peru, Alaska, and Chile. Mummies have also been found in a peat bog in Europe. It was determined that the chemicals in the bog preserved the bodies.

When we think of mummies, we generally think about Egypt, but it wasn't the first civilization to make mummies. It is believed that the Chinchorros of South America may have been the first group of people to intentionally mummify their dead. Scientists have estimated that some of the Chinchorros mummies are over 7,000 years old. The oldest mummy ever found was discovered in a cave in Nevada. It is over 9,000 years old.

In ancient Egypt, millions of people, animals, and even insects were mummified. The more important the deceased had been in life determined how he or she was treated after death. A king or aristocrat was embalmed. His body was smeared with different ointments and was eventually wrapped with linen strips. Peasants were often simply buried in the desert. In either case, the dry climate took the moisture out of the body, and the body became a mummy.

Circle the letter of the answer you believe correctly completes each statement.

1. A bronze disc, which carried a spell, was placed under a mummy's head:
   A. To ward off evil spirits.   B. As an offering to the gods.
   C. As a bribe for grave robbers.   D. To keep it warm.

2. Mummies were buried facing east, so they:
   A. Could see the sun rise.   B. Would face the Nile.
   C. Would face the Sphinx.   D. Were protected from desert winds.

3. When a pet cat died, a family might:
   A. Shave their eyebrows.   B. Offer the cat as a gift to the gods.
   C. Have the cat stuffed.   D. Eat it.

4. Eyes were sometimes painted on the side of the coffin:
   A. To signify royalty.   B. So the mummy could see outside.
   C. As a decoration.   D. To scare grave robbers.

5. During the nineteenth century, mummy heads were:
   A. Thought to be sacred.   B. Declared a national treasure.
   C. Used to make marionettes.   D. Souvenirs and displayed in homes.

6. Ancient Egyptians thought that intelligence was in:
   A. The heart.   B. The brain.
   C. Eye of the beholder.   D. The spleen.

13

Name: _____ Date: _____

The Egyptian Way of Death (cont.)

7. Some tombs contained:
    A. Ostrich mummies.
    B. Potato mummies.
    C. Corn mummies.
    D. Soccer mummies.

8. As far as is known, which of the following have mummies **not** been used for?
    A. Medicine
    B. Paint
    C. Amulets
    D. Fuel

9. In ancient Egypt, a human's life span was:
    A. 9 years.
    B. 29 years.
    C. 39 years.
    D. 49 years.

10. A popular event in Victorian England was:
    A. Mummy burnings.
    B. Unwrapping mummies.
    C. Mummifying animals.
    D. Actors reading the "Book of the Dead."

11. The Egyptians had:
    A. Pet cemeteries.
    B. Athletic contests at funerals.
    C. Cremation Sundays.
    D. An atlas of the underworld.

12. When a mummy was dried out, it would shrink. In order to prevent the body from shrinking, it was sometimes filled with _____ or linen.
    A. Papyrus
    B. Fur
    C. Sawdust
    D. Palm leaves

13. Who built the pyramids?
    A. Hired workers
    B. Volunteers
    C. Slaves
    D. Priests

14. The sarcophagus of the last Egyptian pharaoh was taken to Alexandria where the Greeks:
    A. Used it as a bathtub.
    B. Sailed it down the Nile.
    C. Used it as a bed for Nero.
    D. Displayed it in the Acropolis.

15. The workers who took the dead bodies and turned them into mummies were called:
    A. Embalmers.
    B. Undertakers.
    C. Death surgeons.
    D. Transitioners.

16. The workers who took the dead bodies and turned them into mummies would work on the bodies in a place they called the:
    A. Grand temple.
    B. House of the dead.
    C. House of Styx.
    D. Beautiful house.

Name: _____ Date: _____

The Egyptian Way of Death (cont.)

17. Pyramids had everything that a king might need in his afterlife. Which of the following has
     not been found in a pyramid?
     A. Food and drink   B. Toilet
     C. Eye makeup   D. Live slaves

18. Pharaohs were often buried with a book of the dead that was called:
     A. Destiny.   B. Sleep, Sleep.
     C. Death Be Not Proud.   D. The Book of the Divine Cow.

19. During the nineteenth and twentieth centuries, Egyptian mummies were dug up and sold:
     A. By the ton.   B. Illegally.
     C. To medical schools.   D. For Halloween decorations.

20. How long did it take to make a mummy?
     A. Seven hours   B. Seven days
     C. Seven weeks   D. Seventy days

21. When a man died in ancient Egypt, the women in his family would:
     A. Celebrate.   B. Arrange a marriage for his widow.
     C. Smear their faces with mud.   D. Dress in yellow.

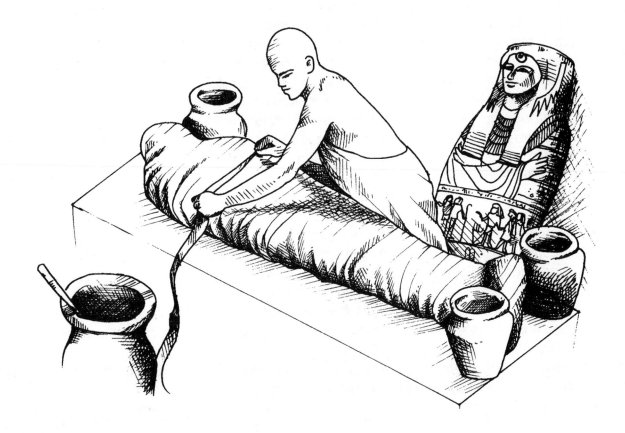

The Egyptian Way of Death Answers

1   **D. Keep it warm.**

2. **A. Could see the sun rise.**

3. **A. Shave their eyebrows.** Cats were sacred, and anyone who killed a cat could be put to death. When a pet cat died, it was mummified, placed in a coffin, and buried. The family might shave their eyebrows (not the cat's eyebrows, their own) as a way to honor its pet. In the nineteenth century, about 300,000 cat mummies found in tombs were taken to England, where they were used as fertilizer in gardens.

4. **B. So the mummy could see outside.**

5. **D. Souvenirs and displayed in homes.**

6. **A. The heart.** Egyptians did not understand the importance of the brain. They felt that the heart controlled feelings, thoughts, and everything else. When preparing the mummy, the embalmers removed the brain but left the heart. It was important that the heart be left inside the body, since they believed that the heart contained a record of the good and bad deeds of the person who had died. According to their religion, Anubis, who was the protector of mummies, would take the heart of the deceased person and put it on a scale. On the other side of the scale was a feather worn in a headdress of a goddess. If the heart balanced perfectly with the feather, the person's soul received eternal life. Those whose hearts did not balance had their hearts thrown to Ammit, a monster known as the "Devourer of the Dead."

7. **C. Corn mummies.** Corn mummies looked like real mummies, but inside the wrapped linen were grains of corn. A corn mummy had a mask of Osiris. The purpose of the corn mummy was to help the spirit of the deceased join Osiris in the afterlife.

8. **C. Amulets.** Over the years, people have used mummies for many different purposes. One strange use for mummies was as a medicine. From the Middle Ages until the seventeenth century, Egyptian mummies were ground up and mixed with other ingredients to cure sick people. People felt that mummies could cure all sorts of diseases and injuries, including poisoning and broken bones. A French king once took a mixture of ground-up mummy and other ingredients in order to heal a wound; as a result, he became very sick. Ground-up mummies were also used to make a brown paint for artists. In the sixteenth century, Egyptians would sometimes burn mummies as fuel. In the eighteenth and nineteenth centuries, Egyptian mummies were purchased by papermaking factories. The bandages that were used to wrap the Egyptian mummies were used to make paper. The bandages did not make a good, high-quality paper for stationery but were used to make a coarse brown paper often used in grocery stores or by butchers to wrap meat. An epidemic of cholera, which was a very serious and sometimes deadly disease, resulted.

9. **B. 29 years.** This is an average. Since there was a high infant mortality rate, which means many children died of accidents and diseases, this brought down the average life expectancy. In fact, if a person survived childhood and became an adult, he or she might expect to live to be around 50 years old.

10. **B. Unwrapping mummies.** Tickets were sold and people would come to see a doctor unwrap a mummy. Refreshments were even served.

The Egyptian Way of Death Answers (cont.)

11. **A. Pet cemeteries.** Animals were identified with certain gods and were often mummified and buried in what today we would call "pet cemeteries." They were also buried in tombs with humans. Egyptians believed that animals acted as messengers to the gods. Mummies of bulls, baboons, birds, cats, jackals, calves, and crocodiles have been found.

12. **C. Sawdust.**

13. **A. Hired workers.** For many years people thought that tombs for royal families were built by slaves. This is not true. Royal families hired the best and most respected builders to build their tombs. Tomb-builders were very well paid and had good working conditions. In fact, the world's first recorded labor strike occurred in ancient Egypt by tomb-builders who were not paid on time. They wouldn't work and kept shouting, "We are hungry!"

14. **A. Used it as a bathtub.**

15. **A. Embalmers.**

16. **D. Beautiful house.**

17. **D. Live slaves.** They would have died thousands of years ago! In addition to food, toys, musicians with their instruments, women, eye makeup, and toilets, there were small model boats to carry the deceased to the kingdom of Osiris.

18. **D. The Book of the Divine Cow.**

19. **A. By the ton.** They were sometimes sold by the graveyard.

20. **D. Seventy days.** First they removed the internal organs and put them in jars. The body was washed in palm wine and covered with natron, a salt, that absorbed the moisture. Forty days later, the body was rubbed with oils, and repacked with sawdust and linen and was then wrapped with linen bandages with charms between the strips. The mummy was then placed in a case.

21. **C. Smear their faces with mud.** They would smear their heads and faces with mud and go through the city beating themselves and ripping off their clothes. When Egyptians left the country, they would take a small, stone model of themselves. If they died before they returned, these models would be sent back to Egypt for burial.

Name: _____ Date: _____

Egyptian Pharaohs

The ancient Egyptians considered the Pharaohs god-kings. As god-kings, the Pharaohs had to dress, eat, and act in special ways. It was felt that every good thing that happened to Egypt was a gift from the king. The people of Egypt worshiped the Pharaohs even after they died.

Circle the letter of the answer you believe correctly completes each statement.

1. The king was not called by his given name or even by the title of "king". Since the king was considered a god, it was insulting to refer to him by name. Instead, he was referred to as "pharaoh." Pharaoh meant:
   A. Palace.
   B. God.
   C. Father.
   D. Son of God.

2. The pharaoh was considered a god on Earth. Anything he said was to be considered as a decree from the god himself. In order to keep the king above the rest of humans, the pharaoh's blood had to be pure, so it was common for a king to:
   A. Marry his sister or half-sister.
   B. Never marry.
   C. Marry royalty from another country.
   D. Never have children.

3. What the pharaohs did and how they dressed were determined by:
   A. Themselves.
   B. Ritual and tradition.
   C. Priests.
   D. The Book of the Living.

4. After an Egyptian king had ruled for about 30 years, there was a festival called the Hebsed Festival. During this festival, the king was required to:
   A. Marry.
   B. Sacrifice 30 young women.
   C. Prove his strength.
   D. Announce a yearly suspension of taxes.

5. Which of the following was **not** a responsibility of the king?
   A. Commanding the Nile to flood
   B. Commanding the sun to rise
   C. Inspecting military outposts
   D. Leading prayer

6. The kings of Egypt were:
   A. Men.
   B. Women.
   C. Men and women.
   D. From the same family.

7. When King Tut died, his widow married:
   A. Her uncle.
   B. Her grandfather.
   C. A Hittite prince.
   D. Tut's brother.

8. Cleopatra was **not**:
   A. An Egyptian.
   B. A Greek.
   C. Unattractive.
   D. Smart.

Egyptian Pharaohs Answers

1. **A. Palace.** Pharaoh meant "palace" or "great house." He was given this name because the king's body was considered to be the house of God.

2. **A. Marry his sister or half-sister.**

3. **B. Ritual and tradition.** Because kings were considered gods, one might think they were able to dress any way they chose and do anything they wanted. This isn't true. What a king wore was a result of tradition, rather than preference. The king would wear both a white and red crown to symbolize both upper and lower Egypt, which was unified. He wore a long gown with a representation of a bull's tail that hung down from the belt. On top of the King's head was another symbol of the king: an ornament in the shape of a female cobra. Kings also carried a shepherd's staff which indicated that they were leading the nation. The king's life was dictated by tradition. His days were heavily scheduled with public ceremonies and rituals.

4. **C. Prove his strength.** He needed to prove that he was strong enough to still be king. Therefore, he had to complete running around a fixed course.

5. **D. Leading prayer.** One of the duties of the king was to make offerings to the gods, imploring them to have the sun rise that day. If the sun did not rise, the Egyptians thought the world would end. Another duty performed by the king was to command the Nile River to rise and flood the land each year. After the land was flooded and the water receded, a layer of rich, fertile soil was left behind; this was needed to grow crops.

6. **C. Men and women.** Although most of the kings of Egypt were men, there were some women who ruled Egypt. When a woman ruled, she was still considered a king, not a queen, although today we sometimes refer to Cleopatra as a queen. Since the king of Egypt was considered to be the **son** of God, it follows that the king must be a man. One woman who was king was Hatshepsut. She would sometimes dress in men's clothing and put on a fake beard to give the impression that she was a man.

7. **B. Her grandfather.** Akhenaten was not a good king. He spent most of his time thinking about religion and other things rather than thinking about protecting Egypt from its enemies. This worried the king's advisers, and Akhenaten died in a very mysterious way. Akhenaten's uncle, Ay, was a high-ranking official and helped arrange for Akhenaten's younger brother, Tutankhamun, to become king. Since King Tut was only nine years old, Ay, his uncle, helped him rule. When Tut died at the age of 18, Uncle Ay worried that he would lose his power, so he decided to marry the widow of King Tut and become king himself. Unfortunately, Tut's widow was Ay's granddaughter, and she did not want to marry grandpa. Instead, she planned to marry the son of a Hittite king. As the young Hittite prince traveled to marry the young widow, he was murdered. The widow had no other choice but to marry her grandfather. Ay then became king. He only lived for about four more years.

8. **A. An Egyptian.** She was a cunning, witty, and charming Greek. Alexander the Great conquered Egypt in 332 B.C., and the Greek Ptolemy family ruled the country for about 300 years. The last ruling member of the Ptolemy family was Cleopatra. Unlike the movies most of us have seen, she was not beautiful. Roman coins, which Marc Antony had had made in her honor, showed that she had a heavy face with a hook nose.

Name: _____ Date: _____

Find the Pharaoh

Pharaohs were afraid that their tombs would be broken into by grave robbers and plundered for their treasures. As a result, bodies were often concealed, and maze-like passages were built to confuse those who entered. Shown below is a pyramid of a pharaoh. Starting at the top of the pyramid, can you navigate the passages so you can get to the king's sarcophagus (the outer coffin)? Beware! If you make a wrong turn, you may be surprised by a poisonous snake or spider.

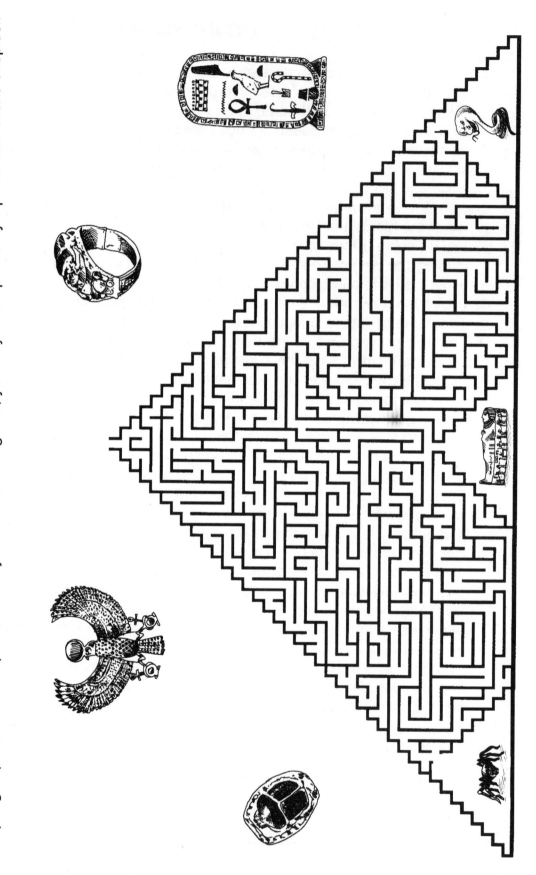

Name: _____ Date: _____

Greek Life

It is believed that the first Greek-speaking peoples migrated into the Balkan Peninsula sometime before 2200 B.C., during the Aegean Bronze Age. By about 800 B.C., a new and important civilization was established in Greece. Ideas about government, art, and philosophy that had originated in Greece were adopted by other countries and still influence the world today. Ancient Greece was organized into small, independent city-states. The most important city-states were Athens and Sparta.

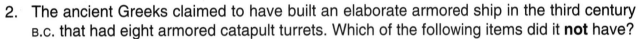

Circle the letter of the answer you believe correctly completes each statement.

1. The Greeks believed that they could tell the future by examining:
    A. The intestines of dead birds.
    B. The moon and stars.
    C. Lamb bones.
    D. Grape leaves.

2. The ancient Greeks claimed to have built an elaborate armored ship in the third century B.C. that had eight armored catapult turrets. Which of the following items did it **not** have?
    A. A pool
    B. A temple
    C. Water cannons
    D. Gardens

3. In the sixth century B.C., there lived a Greek named Aesop who would tell fables that had a moral. Eventually, the priests:
    A. Made him a god.
    B. Made him the chief priest.
    C. Made him pay a fable tax.
    D. Threw him off a cliff.

4. After a Spartan woman was married, she:
    A. Wore a veil.
    B. Cut off her hair and dressed like a man.
    C. Could never leave her house.
    D. Wore a silver ring through her nose.

5. In ancient Sparta, children were considered part of the state. When a child turned seven years old, he was sent to live with a group of other children that was called:
    A. The herd.
    B. Kindergarten.
    C. The school.
    D. Intramurals.

6. As part of their military training, young Spartans were taught to:
    A. Grow vegetables.
    B. Kill and cook wild bear.
    C. Steal food.
    D. Fish.

7. Spartans were brave and excellent fighters. They were trained to keep silent and not cry out in pain. If a Spartan soldier cried out in pain or anguish as he was fighting, he would be punished. In addition:
    A. He was exiled.
    B. His best friend would be punished.
    C. He became a slave.
    D. His family disowned him.

Name: _____ Date: _____

Greek Life (cont.)

8. Spartans proved their bravery, as well as their devotion to the gods by:
   A. Fighting without weapons.
   B. Fasting before a battle.
   C. Being whipped.
   D. Killing those who worshipped other gods.

9. The people who lived in Athens were much different from those who lived in Sparta. Spartans were very tough and warlike, while Athenians preferred the arts. Athenians also had temples and worshipped their own gods. They would sometimes offer the gods sacrifices. One ritual involved killing an ox and offering it up as a sacrifice to the gods. After this ritual, they held a trial in order to determine:
   A. Who killed the ox.
   B. What should be sacrificed next.
   C. Who was the most religious.
   D. Which god was the most powerful.

10. Which of the following weapons did the Greeks invent?
    A. Boomerang
    B. Shield
    C. Flame-thrower
    D. Crossbow

11. The Greeks would go to oracles to find out what the future held. An oracle is a person, often a priest or priestess, through whom a god was believed to speak. The Corinth Oracle was also very famous because:
    A. His predictions were always accurate.
    B. The people could hear the gods speak.
    C. The people thought he was a god.
    D. He had won an Olympic race.

12. The Greeks believed that spirits on their way to heaven:
    A. Rode on a shooting star.
    B. Rested on the moon.
    C. Would stop to watch the Olympics.
    D. Were transported by birds.

13. In Attica, a region of ancient Greece, young women prepared themselves for life and marriage by going into the woods, running, dancing nude, and by pretending to be:
    A. Men.
    B. She-bears.
    C. Hunters.
    D. Goddesses.

14. Evil spirits were feared by the Greeks. They believed that in order to keep an evil spirit from getting into your house, you could:
    A. Have a priest bless the house.
    B. Keep a black canary in the house.
    C. Have a statue of Zeus by the door.
    D. Paint tar around the door.

15. A famous Greek teacher, Pythagoras, was a mathematician and philosopher. Those who followed his beliefs were called Pythagoreans. Which one of the following was **not** a rule of the Pythagoras religion?
    A. Don't eat beans.
    B. Don't stand on your fingernail clippings.
    C. Don't walk along the main street.
    D. Don't pray in public.

Name: _____ Date: _____

Greek Life (cont.)

16. Archestratus was a Greek who wrote the first cookbook in Europe. It was written:
    A. In verse.
    B. In Latin.
    C. On stone.
    D. On human skin.

17. There were vegetarians in ancient Greece. A vegetarian is someone who does not eat meat. When the ancient Greek vegetarians wanted to make a sacrifice to the gods, they would sacrifice:
    A. Vegetables.
    B. Lambs.
    C. Nothing.
    D. Fish.

18. After the Greeks sacrificed an animal to the gods, they would:
    A. Cook and eat the sacrificial animal.
    B. Cremate the remains of the sacrifice.
    C. Give the sacrifice to the priests to eat.
    D. Bury the remains of the sacrifice.

19. After a Greek child was born, the father would inspect him or her. If the baby was a boy and he was fit, the parents might keep him. However, if they had too many other boys, or if the baby was a girl and they could not afford to raise her, they might decide not keep the baby and would:
    A. Offer the child for adoption.
    B. Put the child in a pot on a hill to die.
    C. Donate the child to a temple.
    D. Sacrifice the child to a god.

20. If a father decided to keep a newborn child, he might test the baby's strength by:
    A. Leaving the child in the courtyard overnight.
    B. Throwing the child into the river.
    C. Rubbing the child with icy water, wine, or urine.
    D. Feeding the child feta cheese.

21. When a Greek baby was seven days old, there was a ceremony. The house was swept and sprinkled with water. The family sang hymns, while the father held the baby up and:
    A. Ran around the hearth.
    B. Offered the child's soul to the gods.
    C. Prayed for a long and happy life.
    D. Recited an oath of allegiance to the state.

22. When the Romans were attacking Syracuse in 211 B.C., Archimedes, a scientist and mathematician, devised a weapon that drove the Romans off. The weapon was a(n):
    A. Wild dog.
    B. Mirror system.
    C. Oil cannon.
    D. Five-bladed sword.

23. Although girls did not go to school, boys did. Whenever a boy went to school, he would always take a slave with him. If the boy did not behave:
    A. The slave was sent home.
    B. The teacher would beat the slave.
    C. The slave could beat the student.
    D. The slave was killed.

24. Which of the following games were **not** invented by the Greeks?
    A. Yo-yos
    B. Spinning tops
    C. Puppets moved by strings
    D. Hula hoops

Greek Life Answers

1. **A. The intestines of dead birds.**
2. **C. Water cannons.** It also had a gymnasium.
3. **D. Threw him off a cliff.**
4. **B. Cut off her hair and dressed like a man.**
5. **A. The herd.** Members of the herd were trained to become strong warriors. They were encouraged to fight with each other in order to see who was the strongest. The best fighter became the leader of the group.
6. **C. Steal food.** The children were given little food and were hungry most of the time. Part of their training was to steal food. If they were caught, they were beaten. They weren't beaten because they were stealing but because they were caught.
7. **B. His best friend would be punished.**
8. **C. Being whipped.** They were whipped at the altar of the goddess Artemis. Sometimes, it was a contest among several Spartans in order to determine who was the toughest. Each would be whipped at the altar, and the one who received the most lashes was considered the toughest. Sometimes this activity resulted in death.
9. **A. Who killed the ox.**
10. **C. Flame-thrower.** A tall, straight tree with the branches cut off would be split down the middle. The two halves of the trunk would be hollowed out and then joined back together. At the end of the trunk would be hung a metal pot filled with burning coals, tar, and sulphur. At the other end of the trunk was placed a bellows. When the bellows was operated, there would be a stream of air making the coals grow hotter and a flame to shoot off of them. This weapon was used to burn down walls and doors so a Greek army could enter. Since enemy soldiers standing on a wall above could use bows and arrows and javelins to kill the soldiers operating the bellows, the flame-thrower was encased on a cart with a huge roof that protected the soldiers from weapons above. The soldiers would roll the flame thrower to the wall, squeeze the bellows, the flame would shoot out from the flame thrower, burn down the wall, and the soldiers could enter.
11. **B. The people could hear the gods speak.** At Corinth, a person could actually speak to a god and could hear the god answer back. The Greeks believed that the temple at Corinth was a holy place, but archaeologists have learned that the Corinth Oracle had help, not from the gods, but from builders of the temple. A priest would hide in a tunnel underneath the altar, listen to the visitors' questions, and then shout out the answer through a tube, which echoed and increased the volume of his voice.
12. **B. Rested on the moon.** They also believed that birds delivered messages between heaven and earth.
13. **B. She-bears.**
14. **D. Paint tar around the door.** They believed that evil spirits would stick to tar and not be able to get into the house.
15. **D. Don't pray in public.** Pythagoras believed that when a person died, his soul went to live in another person or living thing. Those who shared his belief worried that if they killed an animal, it might be a relative who had died. They also believed that if they led

Greek Life Answers (cont.)

a good life, they would be reincarnated as a great person. If they led a bad life, they might come back as a disgusting creature, such as a snake or even a woman. Those who believed in the Pythagoras religion had these rules: Don't stand on your fingernail clippings. You could help someone load something but not help him unload it. They were not supposed to eat beans, touch fire with an iron poker, and were not allowed to walk along a main street. They were also not supposed to eat the heart of an animal, look in the mirror beside a lamp, or to leave the mark of their body on a bed when they rose from the bed.

16. **A. In verse.** Scholars believe that since it was written in verse, it was used not only to record recipes, but was meant to be recited.

17. **A. Vegetables.**

18. **A. Cook and eat the sacrificial animal.** The Greeks, as well as other ancient cultures, sacrificed animals to the gods. However, the Greeks did something that many of the other cultures did not do; after they sacrificed the animal to a god, they would roast the animal and eat it. It was considered an honor to eat the liver, kidney, or lungs of a sacrificed animal. After all of the meat was eaten, the blood and fat of the remainder of the sacrifice was mixed together and put into the bladder of the animal. This was then roasted and eaten.

19. **B. Put the child in a pot on a hill to die.** Sometimes a couple who did not have children would go to the hillside, find the baby and adopt him or her before he or she died from the cold or was eaten by wild animals.

20. **C. Rubbing the child with icy water, wine, or urine.** The test was to see if the child was strong enough to survive. Those who survived would be considered a family member, and the birth of a boy would be announced by putting an olive branch on the door. A piece of wool on the door meant the new baby was a girl.

21. **A. Ran around the hearth.**

22. **B. Mirror system.** Archimedes, a prominent Greek mathematician and inventor, lived between 287 and 212 B.C. He studied the areas and volumes of curved solid figures, the areas of plane figures, the principle of the lever, and is given credit for inventing the compound pulley. He also invented the hydraulic screw, which was used to raise water from a lower to a higher level. He is probably best known for discovering the law of physics, usually called Archimedes' Principle. This states that an object immersed in fluid loses weight equal to the weight of the amount of fluid it displaces. When the Romans were attempting to conquer Sicily, Archimedes volunteered to help. It is recorded that he developed the catapult, as well as a system of large mirrors, which reflected and focused the rays of the sun on the Romans' ships. The heat from the reflected sun set the ships on fire and drove off the Romans. Some experts are skeptical of this claim.

23. **C. The slave could beat the student.**

24. **D. Hula hoops.** The following games were invented by Greeks: seesaws, bowling, yo-yos, marionettes, tug-of-war, checkers, dolls with moving parts, baby rattles, and spinning tops.

Name: _____ Date: _____

The Early Olympic Games

The Olympic Games originated at Olympia, a religious center in Greece, in 776 B.C. The Games were held every four years. The period from one Olympic Games to the next was called an Olympiad, and was used by the Greeks to mark time. For example, they would say that some event, such as a death or war, occurred during the third Olympiad. The Olympic Games were not the only national athletic festival in ancient Greece, but they were the best known. The Greeks also participated in the Pythian, Isthmian, and Nemean Games. The Games began simply with just one event and over time included more athletic as well as nonathletic events. Each city-state was invited to join in the celebration, which was designed to honor the god Zeus with sacrifices and athletic contests. The city-states would send their best athletes to compete against each other. Only free and honorable Greek men were permitted to participate in the Games. It was not an international event as it is today. The Olympic Games remained popular until A.D. 394, when the Roman emperor Theodosius I suppressed them.

In 1896, a Frenchman, Pierre de Coubertin, helped to start what we now call the modern Olympics. Since 1896, the modern Olympics have been held every four years. However, because of World War I and World War II, there were no Olympics in the years 1916, 1940, or 1944.

Circle the letter of the answer you believe correctly completes each statement.

1. Olympic athletes originally wore:
   A. Loin cloths.   B. Nothing.
   C. Thongs.   D. Skirts.

2. When a winner in the Olympics returned to his hometown, he would often enter:
   A. Through a hole in the wall.   B. On the back of a Trojan horse.
   C. Carried by other athletes.   D. On a path of flower petals.

3. In modern relay races, runners carry and pass off batons. Originally, the runners carried:
   A. Real bats.   B. Scrolls.
   C. Torches.   D. The bones of defeated enemies.

4. One event in the ancient Olympics was called hoplite racing, where all the contestants:
   A. Would hop.   B. Were blindfolded.
   C. Had originally been slaves.   D. Wore full armor and carried weapons.

5. If there was a war between one or more of the Greek city-states during an Olympic year:
   A. Those at war could not participate.   B. There was a truce until after the games.
   C. The Olympics were cancelled.   D. Separate games were held.

6. Olympic athletes who cheated were:
   A. Beheaded.   B. Enslaved.
   C. Forced to buy statues.   D. Exiled.

The Early Olympic Games (cont.)

7. In the ancient Olympics, which of the following was not an event?
   A. Public speaking
   B. Music
   C. Marathon
   D. Theatre

8. The goddess of victory who watched over the athletic contests was known as:
   A. Nike.
   B. Adidas.
   C. Reebok.
   D. B.U.M.

9. Jumpers often held this when they jumped:
   A. An olive branch
   B. A coin with the image of Zeus
   C. A sprig of parsley
   D. Lead weights

10. Before an Olympic contest, a Greek wrestler named Milon would put a young bull on his shoulders and walk around the stadium to demonstrate his strength. He then would:
    A. Butt the bull with his head until it died.
    B. Kill the bull and bathe in his blood.
    C. Throw the bull at his opponent.
    D. Kill and eat the entire bull.

11. Olympic winners were awarded:
    A. A wreath of olive branches.
    B. A gold medal.
    C. A seat in the Senate.
    D. One hundred lambs.

12. Sporting events were held at religious festivals and at:
    A. The Winter Solstice.
    B. The end of a war.
    C. Toga parties.
    D. Funerals.

13. Married women and slaves were not allowed to participate or attend the games. If a woman viewed the Olympic games, she could be:
    A. Beheaded.
    B. Exiled.
    C. Forced to become a teacher.
    D. Pushed off a cliff.

14. The winner of the chariot races was the:
    A. Driver.
    B. Horse.
    C. Owner of the horse.
    D. Trainer of the horse.

15. The ancient Olympics had a rugged event called the pancratium that combined boxing and wrestling. Every maneuver was allowed in this event except biting and:
    A. Swearing.
    B. Gouging out the opponent's eyes.
    C. Choking.
    D. Praying.

16. During one pancratium match, the winner was:
    A. A woman.
    B. A slave.
    C. A dead man.
    D. Plato.

The Early Olympic Games Answers

1. **B. Nothing.** Except for the chariot and the hoplite races, athletes were nude when they participated in the games. They would put a film of oil over their bodies, and when the games were over, they would clean their skin with bronze scrapers. *Gymnos* is a Greek word meaning "naked." Gymnasium means "where one exercises naked." Fortunately for the athletes, this was before there was a Winter Olympics, which began in 1924.

2. **A. Through a hole in the wall.** When someone from their city won the Olympics, the people would be so proud that they would often break a hole in the city wall so the winner could enter.

3. **C. Torches.** This event is based on a Greek legend. According to the legend, the god Prometheus stole fire from the gods, brought it to earth, and presented it to the humans as a gift. In order for the humans to escape from the gods, they needed to carry the fire on torches and then pass the torches to one another. When the relay race was introduced into the ancient Olympics, torches were used, and if the flame went out, the team lost. Today, of course, batons are used instead of torches.

4. **D. Wore full armor and carried weapons.** A hoplite was an armed infantry soldier in ancient Greece.

5. **B. There was a truce until after the games.**

6. **C. Forced to buy statues.** Athletes who cheated or broke the rules were fined, and the money from the fines was used to build statues of the gods to be placed in front of the stadium. If the athletes who cheated could not afford to pay their fine, their family or their native town had to pay the fine for them.

7. **C. Marathon.** The marathon became an Olympic event in the modern Olympics to honor the memory of Pheidippides, a Greek soldier. In 490 B.C., he ran from the battlefield of Marathon to Athens, a distance of about 22 miles or 35 km.

8. **A. Nike.**

9. **D. Lead weights.** The jumping event was judged for distance, not height. There was no high-jumping event in the ancient Olympics. Jumpers held lead or stone weights. They would swing the weights forward when they jumped in order to increase their distance. As they were landing, they would swing the weights backwards for more thrust.

10. **D. Kill and eat the entire bull.** It took him all day to eat the whole bull.

11. **A. A wreath of olive branches.** Each of the games (Olympic, Pythian, Isthmian, and Nemean games) had their own awards, which by today's standards were very modest. Winners were given wreaths, olive oil, palm branches, laurel leaves, pine needles, and parsley sprigs. However, the adoration heaped upon them by the crowds of admirers more than made up for the small prizes they won. There were banquets in their honor, and, in some cases, statues of the winners were created and placed next to the gods in the temples and at other locations in Olympia. They were celebrated by poets and often lived for the rest of their lives at public expense. They did not have to pay taxes and were allowed to wear purple robes.

12. **D. Funerals.** The Greeks thought the gods and ghosts of the dead enjoyed watching sporting contests.

The Early Olympic Games Answers (cont.)

13. **D. Pushed off a cliff.** Unmarried women were allowed to watch the Games from the stadium. Every four years, women could participate in their own version of the Olympics. Instead of honoring Zeus as the Olympics did, the women's games honored Hera, the wife of Zeus. The women's games were divided into three different age groups and consisted of foot races.

14. **C. Owner of the horse.** It was possible for a woman who owned a horse to win the chariot races, even though she could not attend.

15. **B. Gouging out the opponent's eyes.** In the pancratium, the most rigorous of the sports, the contest continued until one of the participants gave up. What made the contest even more brutal was the fact that there were no weight or size classes in the boxing contests. The largest contestant could be matched up with the smallest.

16. **C. A dead man.** During one pancratium match, one fighter began choking the other as his leg was being twisted. His leg caused him so much pain that he surrendered, just as his opponent died of strangulation. The dead man was proclaimed the winner.

Name: _____ Date: _____

The Modern Olympic Games

The modern Olympic Games began in 1896. Pierre de Coubertin, a Frenchman, suggested the idea of a modern Olympics in 1892 when he spoke at a meeting of the Union des Sports Athlétiques in Paris. Little interest was shown until an international sports congress met in 1894. In this congress, there were representatives and delegates from nine countries who supported the idea. De Coubertin wanted to hold the Olympic Games in France, but the other representatives felt that Greece should be the site of the first modern Olympics. The council agreed that the Olympics would move every four years to other great cities of the world.

Circle the letter of the answer you believe correctly completes each statement.

1. The Olympic flame in Olympia, Greece is rekindled every two years by using:
   A. A fire from the temple of Zeus.   B. The sun's rays.
   C. An ember from the previous games.   D. A gold-medal winner from Greece.

2. Olympic middleweight medalist Egerton Marcus learned his boxing skills from:
   A. His mother.   B. Reading books.
   C. A nun.   D. Theodore Roosevelt.

3. What did Olympians Shun Fujimoto, Kerry Strug and Joe Frazier all have in common? They all:
   A. Were boxers.   B. Won a gold medal
                                                while injured.
   C. Participated without qualifying.   D. Had the same coach.

4. What did Olympians Walter "Buddy " Davis, Lis Hartel, and Wilma Rudolph all have in common? They all:
   A. Competed in four Olympics.   B. Practiced running in waist-deep water.
   C. Had polio when they were younger.   D. Were cousins.

5. In 1928, six of the eight entrants in the women's 800-meter race:
   A. Finished at the same time.   B. Were from the same country.
   C. Collapsed at the finish line.   D. Were disqualified.

6. Abebe Bikila, an Ethiopian, was the first man to successfully win two consecutive marathons. His first victory gained a lot of attention because:
   A. He didn't wear shoes.   B. He didn't wear clothes.
   C. He hadn't trained.   D. He was only 14 years old.

7. The distance for the marathon race is 26 miles and 385 yards. This distance was chosen because it is the distance between:
   A. Marathon and Athens.   B. Olympia and Athens.
   C. The Acropolis and Olympic Stadium.   D. Windsor Castle and the Olympic Stadium.

Name: _____ Date: _____

The Modern Olympic Games (cont.)

8. When the Olympic champion Gwen Torrence was in the tenth grade, she set an unofficial state record in the 220 yd dash while wearing:
   A. A dress.
   B. Low-heeled patent leather pumps.
   C. Leg braces.
   D. A mask.

9. Kerstin Palm from Sweden was the first woman to:
   A. Compete in the Olympics.
   B. Compete in seven Olympics.
   C. Beat a man in the Olympics.
   D. Box in the Olympics.

10. When selecting a young female gymnast to coach, the coach will often examine:
    A. Her father's finances.
    B. Her pulse rate.
    C. Teenage pictures of her mother.
    D. The circumference of her head.

11. The oldest person to win an Olympic medal was Oscar Swahn. How old was he?
    A. 42
    B. 56
    C. 64
    D. 72

12. During the 1900 Olympics, most of the athletes competing:
    A. Were from the United States.
    B. Didn't know they were in the Olympics.
    C. Were women.
    D. Were left-handed.

13. During the 1900 Olympics, the hurdles were made of:
    A. Wood.
    B. Plastic.
    C. Broken telephone poles.
    D. Miniature Eiffel Towers.

14. Which of the following was not an event at the 1900 Olympics in Paris?
    A. Fishing
    B. Checkers
    C. Croquet
    D. Pentathlon

15. Since the first Olympic Games were held in 1896, which two countries have participated in every one?
    A. United States and Great Britain
    B. Germany and France
    C. Russia and Italy
    D. Greece and Australia

16. American Myer Prinstein finished runner-up in the 1900 long jump in Paris, despite:
    A. Not having entered the event.
    B. Having the longest jump.
    C. Not showing up for the finals.
    D. The fact his main sport was boxing.

17. The longest wrestling match in Olympic history lasted over:
    A. 3 hours.
    B. 7 hours.
    C. 11 hours.
    D. 15 hours.

Name: _____ Date: _____

The Modern Olympic Games (cont.)

18. When the modern Olympics began in 1896, first-place winners received:
    A. A gold medal.
    B. A silver medal.
    C. A bronze medal.
    D. An oak seedling.

19. The U.S. Olympic Gymnastics team is usually composed of high school students because:
    A. They can practice more.
    B. They are more limber.
    C. They learn faster.
    D. They are shorter.

20. In 1988, before a competition, the Korean Judo team would:
    A. Go to a temple and pray.
    B. Go to a cemetery and sit alone.
    C. Stand on their heads.
    D. Watch Jackie Chan movies.

21. In the 1896 Olympics, the singles tennis match was won by:
    A. A spectator.
    B. A woman.
    C. A married man.
    D. The King of Norway.

22. In 1908, the Russian team arrived late and did not participate because:
    A. Their ship was torpedoed.
    B. They were using a different calendar.
    C. They had to sneak out of the country.
    D. In Russian, "July" means September.

23. In the 1904 Olympics in St. Louis, there was a:
    A. Men's Heavyweight Judo event
    B. Underwater Race
    C. Men's Single Rowing event
    D. Juggling event

24. What did Olympians, swimmer Johnny Weismuller, shot-putter Herman Brix, swimmer Buster Crabbe, and decathalete Glenn Morris all have in common?
    A. They were from the same city.
    B. They were classmates in college.
    C. They all became models.
    D. They all played Tarzan in the movies.

25. After Hungarian Karoly Takacs, a member of the 1930 Hungarian National Rapid-Fire Pistol Shooting Team, lost his shooting hand when a grenade exploded, he still wanted to be in the Olympics. He eventually won an Olympic gold medal in:
    A. Pistol shooting.
    B. Figure skating.
    C. Marathon.
    D. Diving.

26. Dan Jensen was a speed skater. Which statement about him is **not** true?
    A. He only won one Olympic race.
    B. He competed in four Olympic Games.
    C. He was favored for most of his races.
    D. He never set a world record.

27. Who won seven medals, each one in world-record time, at a single Olympics?
    A. Jim Thorpe
    B. Tiger Woods
    C. Michael Jordan
    D. Mark Spitz

The Modern Olympic Games Answers

1. **B. The sun's rays.** Using a concave reflective mirror and the sun's rays, the Olympic flame is rekindled every two years. Providing, of course, the skies are not cloudy.

2. **A. His mother.** She was a former welterweight boxer.

3. **B. Won a gold medal while injured.** In 1976, **Shun Fujimoto** broke his kneecap while performing in the floor exercise. The next day, for the sake of his team, he performed a near perfect routine on the rings and even stuck the landing. He held his position until he was judged and then collapsed in pain. The Japanese team beat the Soviet Union by just four-tenths of a point.

    Since the USSR had begun coming to the games in 1952, they had never lost a women's team gymnastics competition in the Olympics; after the USSR was dissolved, the Russians continued winning until 1996 at Atlanta. The American team was in the lead and only needed a good performance on the vault to beat the Russians. However, the Americans began to falter. One by one they fell, could not stick their landings, and drew low scores.

    The outcome was in doubt. The final performer for the Americans was **Kerry Strug**, a national vaulting champion. She had two chances to make a good vault and to land flat on both feet. On her first vault she went out too fast, landed on her back, and a loud pop was heard coming from her ankle. Kerry was in severe pain, but she limped back, said a prayer, ran down the mat, executed an excellent vault, and landed on both feet, ignoring her pain. She held her pose until she was judged, and then collapsed. Her performance had wrapped up the championship for the United States.

    Joe Frazier's Olympic boxing career initially began when he **didn't** make the Olympic team. At the Olympic trials, he lost a close fight, and his opponent was selected for the Olympics. However, an official of the AAU suggested that Frazier make the journey to Tokyo to be an alternate, in the event that someone got hurt; Frazier decided to make the trip. However, before making the trip, he fought an exhibition match with the heavyweight who was to fight in the Olympics. The heavyweight broke his wrist during the bout and could not fight, so Frazier was selected to take his place. During the Olympics, he easily won his preliminary rounds. In the semifinals, he fought a very strong and favored Soviet boxer and hit him so hard that not only was the fight stopped, but Frazier broke his thumb. Frazier did not tell anyone, because he wanted to fight in the finals. In spite of the injury, Joe did fight in the finals, favoring his left hand with the broken thumb, and he was declared the winner. "Smok'n Joe" Frazier went on to become the undisputed heavyweight champion of the world.

4. **C. Had polio when they were younger.** When the American Olympian **Walter "Buddy" Davis** was a boy, he was diagnosed with polio, a dreaded disease that cripples and paralyzes. Today children take a vaccine that has almost eliminated polio from the face of the earth. Davis was bedridden for a long time but was eventually able to walk with braces on both legs and on his right arm. As he became older, he was able to give up the braces and use crutches; he then gave the crutches up, and finally walked on his own. For years, he had trouble walking because of poor circulation, so he began running to develop his leg muscles, in spite of the fact that his doctors told him to avoid any type of strenuous activity. By the time he was a senior in high school, he was 6'8"

The Modern Olympic Games Answers (cont.)

tall and weighed 200 pounds. He entered college on a basketball scholarship but eventually became interested in track as a senior in college. He broke the American high-jump record by jumping six feet, eight and one-half inches. This record qualified him for the Olympics where he won the gold medal. In 1953, Davis set a world high-jump record of 6 feet, eleven and one-half inches. He then went to the National Basketball Association and played with the Philadelphia Warriors when they won the NBA championship in 1956. He also played with the St. Louis Hawks when they won the NBA championship in 1958. He played professional basketball for five seasons.

Lis Hartel was a young mother with a two-year-old child when she contracted polio. She was an excellent horsewoman living in Denmark and was one of Scandinavia's best riders. However, riders control a horse not only with their hands and arms, but with their legs as well. The way riders sit, flex their leg muscles, and press with their knees tells a horse exactly what to do. So when Lis contracted polio and the doctor said she would probably never use her legs again, it was thought that she could never ride a horse, much less enter a competition, but Lis was very determined. She exercised hard, and eventually had her friends lift her on top of a horse; however, with her legs paralyzed from the knees down and almost no muscles in her thighs that worked, she was unable to stay on the horse. However, she persisted, and eventually learned to control the horse with her voice and by shifting her weight. In 1952, she entered the Olympic Games; she had to be lowered into the saddle in order to compete and won the silver medal. Four years later, she won the silver medal again.

Wilma Rudolph had polio as a child. The disease left her left leg twisted and bent so badly that it needed to be placed in a brace. She stayed in the brace for two years and then was fitted with a special shoe so she could walk. When she was 11 years old, she wanted to play basketball with her brothers, so she took off the shoe and found that her leg was able to support her weight. She played basketball and other sports in high school. When she was 16 years old, she qualified for the Olympics. She did not win an individual medal in her first Olympics, but her team finished third, and she received a bronze medal. Four years later, she traveled to Rome for the games and was the first American woman to win three gold medals in one Olympics. She set Olympic records in both of her individual races and a world record in the relay. After the Olympics, she set six more world records. Rudolph retired in 1962.

5. **C. Collapsed at the finish line.** They were exhausted because of the heat and poor training. The event was cancelled but reintroduced in 1960.

6. **A. He didn't wear shoes.** The victories came in 1960 in Rome and 1964 in Tokyo. For the second victory, he did wear shoes.

7. **D. Windsor Castle and the Olympic Stadium.** The marathon is a race to commemorate Pheidippides, a Greek soldier who ran from Marathon to Athens in 490 B.C. to tell the Athenians of a battle with the Persians. The distance was about 25 miles over a trail with hills and other obstacles. After he arrived in Athens and told the people that their army was victorious, he died. A marathon of about the same distance was run at the first modern Olympics held in 1896. After that, the marathon was always about 25 miles long. That changed in 1908. The royal family in Britain asked that the marathon

The Modern Olympic Games Answers (cont.)

begin at Windsor Castle so the royal children could see the beginning of the race. The distance from the castle to the stadium was 26 miles and 385 yards or 42,195 meters. The race has remained at this distance.

8. **B. Low-heeled patent leather pumps.**

9. **B. Compete in seven Olympics.**

10. **C. Teenage pictures of her mother.** The coach is interested in how the girl will look when she becomes a teenager, and the girl's mother is the best way to find out. The body shape of the girl will likely be similar to that of her mother.

11. **D. 72.** In 1920, Swedish Olympians Oscar Swahn and his son Alfred won the silver medal in the running deer-shooting event. Oscar was 72 years old, the oldest medal winner in Olympic history. The father and son team competed together in three Olympic Games, 1908, 1912, and 1920. They earned a total of 14 medals—six gold, four silver, and four bronze. Alfred competed a fourth time, in 1924, when he was 45 years old, and won a bronze medal.

12. **B. Didn't know they were in the Olympics.** The Olympics were held in Paris at the same time the city was hosting an international exposition, which was basically a world's fair. The French thought the Olympics would take away from the exposition, so they didn't use the name, "Olympics," but referred to it as an "international championship."

13. **C. Broken telephone poles.** For the reason given in the last answer, the French did little to make these Olympics outstanding. The discus field was so small that the discus landed in the woods. Sprinters ran on grass fields instead of cinders. There were few spectators.

14. **D. Pentathlon.**

15. **D. Greece and Australia.**

16. **C. Not showing up for the finals.** Prinstein did not jump in the finals because it was against his beliefs to participate on Sunday. At this time, qualifying jumps counted, so he took second on the basis of his qualifying jumps.

17. **C. 11 hours.** The Greco-Roman wrestling match in Stockholm in 1912 between Alfred Asikainen, a Finn, and Russian Martin Klein lasted more than 11 hours. When Klein eventually won the match, he was too exhausted to participate in the championship match, so he received the silver.

18. **B. A silver medal.** Medals were not awarded in the ancient Olympics. The first-place winner was given an olive wreath to wear on his head. Those who came in second and third received nothing. When the Modern Olympics were revived in 1896, first-place winners received silver medals. For some reason, gold was considered inferior to silver. At the 1904 games in St. Louis, gold replaced silver for first place. These were real, solid gold medals. The last Olympic medals made entirely out of gold were awarded in 1912. The gold medals today are actually sterling silver covered with a thin coat of pure gold.

19. **A. They can practice more.** While some of the best United States gymnasts are in college, they must follow guidelines set down by the NCAA that say they can only train 20 hours per week. So, most of the Olympic U.S. teams are composed of young women still in high school, because they can train in private gyms with no restrictions.

The Modern Olympic Games Answers (cont.)

20. **B. Go to a cemetery and sit alone.** They would sit alone in a cemetery the night before a match and then return to see videotapes of their competition and to practice.

21. **A. A spectator.** He had not come to the Olympics to participate.

22. **B. They were using a different calendar.** They were still using the Julian Calendar. Most of the world was using the Gregorian Calendar

23. **B. Underwater race.** A gold medal was won by Duke Kahanamoku, a descendant of a Hawaiian chief.

24. **D. They all played Tarzan in the movies.** By far, the best known was Johnny Weismuller. When Johnny was 11 years old, his doctor examined him because he was very frail and sick. The doctor said he had a very weak heart, and one way to strengthen his heart was to swim. Johnny lived in Chicago and could not afford to go to a pool, so he and his brother swam in Lake Michigan. He became stronger, and when he was 17 years old, he set his first world record. Eventually, he would set 50 more world records. At age 18, he was the first person in history to swim 100 meters in less than a minute. He participated in the 1924 and 1928 Olympic Games, where he won gold medals. He also competed with the U.S. water polo team and won a bronze medal. He was planning to participate in the 1932 games and was favored to win his events in these games as well. However, the BVD company hired Johnny to model its swimming suits in magazine ads at a salary of $500 a week for five years. This was a lot of money in 1932, which was the beginning of the Great Depression. By accepting money, he was no longer an amateur and could no longer participate in the Olympic games. He began his movie career in 1932; for the next 16 years, he was Tarzan in the movies. After he gave up the role of Tarzan, three other Olympians became Tarzan. They were shot-putter Herman Brix, swimmer Buster Crabbe, and decathlete Glenn Morris.

25. **A. Pistol shooting.** Hungarian Karoly Takacs was a member of the 1930 Hungarian National Rapid-Fire Pistol Shooting Team that won the European championship. When Hungary was preparing for war, Takacs picked up a grenade that exploded in his hand. The surgeons were able to save his life but not his shooting hand. After the war, Takacs began practicing shooting again. This time he practiced with his left hand; in 1948, he qualified as a member of the Hungarian team. He won first place, and four years later he took first place again. He participated in one more Olympics in 1956 when he was 46 years old. He finished eighth.

26. **D. He never set a world record.** Dan Jensen was a speed skater who competed in the Olympics for 16 years. Although he was a favorite in most of the Olympic Games, it seemed as if some bit of bad luck caused him to lose every time. On one occasion, on the morning he was supposed to race, his sister died; he fell in some races. It wasn't until the last race of his last Olympics that he did win. He not only won a gold medal, but he set a world record.

27. **D. Mark Spitz.** Although Mark Spitz won only a silver and a bronze medal when competing in the 1968 Olympics, he won a record seven gold medals in the 1972 Olympic Games. In the 1972 games, he won the 100- and 200-meter freestyle and butterfly events and was a member of the winning 4x100-meter and the 4x200-meter freestyle relay and the 4x100-meter medley relay teams. He set 32 world records and 38 U.S. swimming records during his career.

Name: _____ Date: _____

The Polybius Checkerboard

Polybius was a Greek historian born in 200 B.C. In 168 B.C., he was taken hostage and sent to Rome. He became friends with a Roman general and accompanied him to Spain and Africa. His history books have 40 volumes. In addition to writing history, Polybius devised a code that is called the Polybius Checkerboard. Since there are 25 spaces in the grid, and as there are 26 letters in our alphabet, two letters have to share the same space.

	1	2	3	4	5
1	A	B	C	D	E
2	F	G	H	I	J
3	K	L	M	N	O
4	P	Q	R	S	T
5	U	V	W	X/Y	Z

Shown below is a secret message for you to decipher using the Polybius Checkerboard. In order to do this, you need to find out which number pair equals which letter. The first number of the pair is in the first column on the left side of the checkerboard. Then go across until you land on the column under the second number of the pair. The letter in the code is where these two number pairs intersect. Here is an example: the number 32 is the letter "L". You will find this by going down the first column until you find the number 3, and then go across until you are under the column with the number 2 at the top. The square where these two numbers meet is the letter "L." The letter 23 is the letter "H."

A Greek Mystery From History in Code

Decode this mystery from history using the Polybius Checkerboard and see if you can answer the question the mystery asks.

The Spartan general Pausanius sent a message to the Persian king saying he was willing to betray Sparta. He was sure the messenger he chose was very loyal and would deliver the message. However, because of something he read in the message, the messenger took it to Sparta instead of to the Persian king.

Question: 53 23 11 45   14 24 14   45 23 15   33 15 44 44 15 34 22 15 43

___ ___ ___ ___   ___ ___ ___   ___ ___ ___   ___ ___ ___ ___ ___ ___ ___ ___ ___

44 15 15   24 34   45 23 15   33 15 44 44 11 22 15?

___ ___ ___   ___ ___   ___ ___ ___   ___ ___ ___ ___ ___ ___ ___

Answer: _____

Name: _____ Date: _____

Roman Life

Italy has almost always been an important center of civilization. Rome, the main city in Italy, developed the largest civilization in the Ancient World. Most of the civilized world was part of the Roman Empire. Territory from what is now Iran to what is now Britain was included in the Roman Empire. They all had the same laws, paid taxes to Rome, and were protected by the Roman army. When the Roman Empire finally fell, many of the nations we know today, such as France, Italy, and England, began to develop.

Circle the letter of the answer you believe correctly completes each statement.

1. Whenever the Romans conquered a country, they would often require the young men of the conquered country to serve in the Roman army. Some would refuse by:
   A. Running away.
   B. Pretending to be insane.
   C. Cutting off their thumbs.
   D. Wearing dresses.

2. The typical theater in Roman times had fast food and:
   A. Slow food.
   B. Showers.
   C. Popcorn.
   D. Snow cones.

3. It is sometimes said that after a battle an army was "decimated." What did the word decimated mean to the Roman army?
   A. They destroyed their enemy.
   B. They killed 10% of their own soldiers.
   C. They made their enemy use decimals.
   D. They made their enemy pay a 10% fine.

4. People who worked in specific trades would form social clubs, which were basically trade unions. One primary purpose of these unions was to:
   A. Provide funerals.
   B. Train apprentices.
   C. Set prices.
   D. Further their chosen profession.

5. At several locations in Rome, there were many public toilets that were:
   A. Free to slaves, but others had to pay.
   B. Only for women.
   C. Only for men.
   D. In full view of the public.

6. When Romans relaxed at the public baths or at the beach, men generally wore a loincloth made of wool or linen, while some of the women wore:
   A. Bikinis.
   B. Nothing.
   C. Togas.
   D. A loincloth made of wool or linen.

7. Which of the following services or activities were **not** available at a Roman bath?
   A. Hairdressing
   B. Wrestling
   C. Leg-waxing
   D. Dominoes

Name: _____ Date: _____

Roman Life (cont.)

8. If a girl was born to a Roman family, the family:
   - A. Celebrated.
   - B. Mourned.
   - C. Arranged for her marriage.
   - D. Sold her into slavery.

9. When the Romans picked their victims for sacrifice, they would say:
   - A. "Eenie, meenie, miny, mo."
   - B. "The Emperor has spoken."
   - C. "The gods have chosen you."
   - D. "You are about to be blest."

10. Which of the following pets would most likely **not** be found in a Roman home?
    - A. Parrots
    - B. Snakes
    - C. Monkeys
    - D. Dogs

11. Girls would be given a name similar to:
    - A. Their mother.
    - B. Their father.
    - C. A goddess.
    - D. Their father's mother.

12. The Romans originated the word *barbarian,* which to them meant anyone who was a:
    - A. Stranger.
    - B. Mongol.
    - C. Greek.
    - D. Lawyer.

13. Which of the following was **not** available at a Roman bathhouse?
    - A. Snack bars
    - B. Gift shops
    - C. Libraries
    - D. Jet baths

14. Every Roman legionnaire went into battle with a:
    - A. Picture of the emperor.
    - B. Small statue of a god.
    - C. Flotation device.
    - D. First-aid kit.

15. The oldest father in the household had authority over everyone else in the household. One of his decisions was whether or not a newborn child should be:
    - A. Given the family name.
    - B. Considered an heir.
    - C. Allowed to live.
    - D. A soldier, merchant, or politician.

16. Which of the following medical procedures did the Romans **not** perform?
    - A. Plastic surgery
    - B. Brain surgery
    - C. Removing tonsils
    - D. Removing gall stones

17. Romans mostly liked to laugh at:
    - A. The misfortune of others.
    - B. Themselves.
    - C. The gods.
    - D. Greek customs.

Name: _____ Date: _____

Roman Life (cont.)

18. The summer home, or as it was sometimes called, the villa, belonging to Pliny the Younger, was about 17 miles from Rome. It was said to be a modest villa with five bedrooms, four dining rooms, a parlor, two drawing rooms, four bathing rooms, a library, servants' quarters, and an adjoining cottage with a bedroom and a study. The house had a large terrace with gardens and even a:
    A. Fish farm.
    B. Tennis court.
    C. Koi pond.
    D. Small zoo.

19. Roman children had many different games they played. One of their favorite games used:
    A. Ram's horns.
    B. Horseshoes.
    C. A pig's bladder.
    D. Chicken beaks.

20. Wigs were popular with Roman women. The wigs were often made of:
    A. Slaves' hair.
    B. Hair from a dead relative.
    C. Wool.
    D. Linen.

21. Rubbish was disposed of by throwing it:
    A. Into a volcano.
    B. Into the road.
    C. Into landfills.
    D. Into the ocean.

22. Ancient Rome had trials that, in some respects, were similar to those we have in the United States. A plaintiff would bring a case to court, and there would be a defendant who was being sued or accused of a crime. There was a judge, and there could be professional lawyers, although sometimes people defended themselves. The guilt or innocence of a defendant was decided by:
    A. The emperor.
    B. The judge.
    C. The chief counsel.
    D. As many as 75 jurors.

23. Some believe that the practice of having people fight until the death actually began:
    A. At athletic games.
    B. At funerals.
    C. In Greece.
    D. In Mesopotamia.

Roman Life Answers

1. **C. Cutting off their thumbs.** Without a thumb, they could not hold a sword to fight; however, the Romans were not easily fooled. If anyone tried to avoid joining the Roman army by cutting off his thumb or by doing anything else to make him ineligible to serve, he was sentenced to death. The Romans would also tattoo or brand those who didn't want to serve in the Roman army, so if they ran away, they could easily be identified.

2. **B. Showers.** Showers allowed the spectators to cool themselves. Roman plays were more violent than Greek plays. In one play, Laureosis, a villain, was supposed to be killed as part of the plot. During the performance, right before the villain is supposed to be killed, the actor playing the part left the stage, and a criminal under the sentence of death was pushed onto the stage. He was mauled and killed by a live bear onstage as the audience screamed in delight.

3. **B. They killed 10% of their own soldiers.** The Roman army was successful because they rarely retreated. Their armies would advance with swords drawn and shields up. If a soldier in the front lines was wounded, those behind him would step in to take his place. If a company of Roman soldiers retreated during a battle, the whole company was punished. Every tenth man of the company was beaten to death with a wooden club. When this happened, it was said that the company was **decimated**.

4. **A. Provide funerals.** The purpose of these clubs or unions was not to train apprentices as they did in medieval times. They had banquets and provided funerals for members who could not afford them. For this reason, slaves often joined these clubs.

5. **D. In full view of the public.** Some contained as many as 60 seats and were along the street in full view of the public. They were not divided into cubicles and provided no privacy. Using a public toilet was not embarrassing to the Romans; they considered these public latrines as meeting places where they could talk to friends.

6. **A. Bikinis.** The bikinis were very similar to those worn today.

7. **D. Dominoes.** The favorite leisure pastime of ancient Romans was to visit the public bath every day or, at a minimum, a few times a week. The bathhouse was a place where people could socialize, exercise, talk, and play games. The fee was so low that even poor people could go. Women and men attended the public bath at different times, and in some cases, there were separate facilities for women and men. In some respects, the ancient Roman bath could be compared to the YMCA or YWCA today. There was a room with benches in

Roman Life Answers (cont.)

which to change clothes and compartments for storing the person's street clothes. The bathers then went into a warm room; when they started to perspire, they went into another room for a hot bath. Then they went into a cold room for a cold bath, and then to a room for a massage with oil. Eventually, the bather returned for his or her clothes. Bathhouses sometimes had a swimming pool and a sauna; some even provided the service of leg-waxing.

8. **B. Mourned.** Roman families generally wanted male children. If a girl was born, the family mourned, and sometimes she would be left outside to die.

9. **A. "Eenie, meenie, miny, mo."** Some experts believe that victims were chosen by using this phrase. In ancient Britain, when shepherds would count their sheep, they would use a numbering system that sounded like "eenie, meenie, miny, mo." The phrase was copied, and it eventually made its way to Rome.

10. **A. Parrots.** Romans had many different kinds of pets in their homes. Some of them were the ordinary types of pets that we have today—dogs, cats, birds, etc. But there were other pets that were a little bit more unusual. Some households had snakes. Snakes were good for killing mice and rats and were also considered a fertility symbol. Snakes represented the spirit of the family. Another type of exotic pet common among the Romans were monkeys. Wild monkeys were captured in Africa and shipped to Rome. They were often kept on leashes so they could not escape. It is unlikely that a parrot could be found in a Roman home. Parrots are generally from tropical regions. Most come from South America, Australia, and New Guinea. Only a few species are native to Africa and mainland Asia.

11. **B. Their father.** The girl's name would be similar to her father's name, but the ending would be changed. If a man's name ended with the letters "us," his daughter's name would end with the letter "a." For example, if a man's name was Claudius, then his daughter's name would be Claudia.

12. **A. Stranger.** The word *barbarian* came about because the Romans could not understand the language of people from other countries. To them, their language sounded like the bleating of sheep. The Romans would say it sounded as if the people were saying, "Bah, Bah, Bah," and eventually the word *barbarian* came into being.

13. **D. Jet baths.** Roman baths had massage parlors, hairdressers, exercise rooms, and gyms. People could wrestle, play handball, or lift weights. There were snack bars, gift shops, libraries, and reading rooms. Many also had gardens where people could relax after their baths. Rome had more than 800 public baths throughout the city.

14. **D. First-aid kit.**

15. **C. Allowed to live.** Just after a birth, the midwife put the child on the ground. If the father picked the child up, it meant the child would live, and the family would raise it. Sometimes a father did not pick up the child, and it was left outside in a deserted spot to die. This practice was known as "exposure." A father might make this decision because the child was handicapped or deformed in some way. Since boys were more sought after by fathers, more girl babies died of exposure than boys. However, not every child who was left outside to die actually did die. Very often, a child who was abandoned was rescued and reared by a childless couple. Others would find a child, raise it, and then sell it into slavery.

Roman Life Answers (cont.)

16. **D. Remove gall stones.** The only scientific thought or research in Roman times was devoted to medicine. Romans could set fractured bones, remove tonsils, and repair hernias. They performed operations, abortions, and did plastic surgery. They made false arms and legs for those people who were missing these body parts and even performed rudimentary brain surgery. Although many doctors had a good knowledge of the human body and how it worked, there were still many who preferred to treat sickness with magic and prayer to their gods.

17. **A. The misfortune of others.** Romans liked to laugh at many things, but their primary source of laughter was about physical features and the misfortunes of others. We would find their brand of humor cruel today. Roman parents even thought it was funny to give their children names that reflected problems the children had. For example, they might call their child pig, lame, fat, stammerer, flatfeet, or other names that we would find insulting today.

18. **B. Tennis court.**

19. **C. A pig's bladder.** After the bladder was cleaned, it was blown up and tossed from one player to another. The object of the game was to keep the bladder in the air.

20. **A. Slaves' hair.** Being well-groomed was so important to the Romans that part of the household staff of many of the rich included a barber. Romans used curling irons to shape their hair. Romans felt that to dress well and to be well-groomed were so important, they were willing to go into debt in order to look good. At one party, for example, a wealthy host was so concerned about looking good that he changed his outfit eleven times during the meal.

21. **B. Into the road.**

22. **D. As many as 75 jurors.**

23. **B. At funerals.** It was thought that those who were dead were pleased with the sacrifice of the others. So, criminals, slaves, or prisoners of war were sometimes sacrificed at a funeral. These kinds of sacrifices became so popular that they began to stage them in huge arenas, rather than at funerals. Gladiators, many of whom were slaves, would sometimes become very well-known. If a slave was a good fighter and won enough contests, it was possible for him to win his freedom. When this happened, he would be given a wooden sword, which was a symbol of freedom.

At the Coliseum in Rome, people could watch animals fighting. There would be elephants, rhinoceroses, and other animals fighting each other and against other species. There were also sea battles. The arena would be flooded, and warships in the arena would be filled with men who would fight each other. In the movies we have often seen armed men fight against tigers, lions, and leopards, but they also fought against other animals, such as elephants. Sometimes, men were not given any weapons at all but had to fight bears with nothing but their hands. On one occasion in ancient Rome, 5,000 animals were killed in one day at the Coliseum. Lions and elephants living in North Africa and the Middle East were used for Roman games.

At the arena, there were also chariot races and animal acts. Tigers, lions, and elephants would perform tricks taught to them by their trainers. In that respect, the circus of ancient Rome would be similar to the circuses we know today.

Name: _____ Date: _____

Roman Customs and Superstitions

Circle the letter of the answer you believe correctly completes each statement.

1. Romans considered _____ unlucky.
   A. Black cats
   B. A rabbit's foot
   C. The left side of anything
   D. Whistling after midnight

2. When a farmer wanted to cut down trees in a certain spot, he would:
   A. See who owned the land.
   B. Ask permission from a priest.
   C. Sacrifice a pig.
   D. Pay a fee to the emperor.

3. In order to enjoy a feast a little longer, a guest would sometimes:
   A. Take a nap at the table.
   B. Chew on coffee beans.
   C. Vomit.
   D. Take a bath between courses.

4. In order to protect themselves from the "evil eye," fire, storm, poison, and other evils, Romans would decorate their houses with:
   A. Statues of gods.
   B. Written prayers.
   C. Holly.
   D. Mirrors.

5. The Romans felt that each family had a special guardian spirit known as:
   A. Ben Hur.
   B. Cecil.
   C. Ariel.
   D. Genius.

6. In ancient Rome, it was considered a sign of leadership to be born:
   A. With a crooked nose.
   B. With large feet.
   C. Under a full moon.
   D. Of parents who were over 30 years old.

7. When a guest was enjoying a feast at a banquet, he would sometimes:
   A. Soak the food in wine.
   B. Kiss his host.
   C. Light a Roman candle.
   D. Go to the bathroom at the table.

8. When a member of the family died, someone was often hired to:
   A. Give a funeral speech.
   B. Write his biography.
   C. Impersonate the dead person.
   D. Write a song about him.

9. When Romans ate, they:
   A. Sat at a table.
   B. Sat on the floor.
   C. Reclined on a couch.
   D. Stood up.

Name: _____ Date: _____

Roman Customs and Superstitions (cont.)

10. When dining at someone's home, it was considered polite for a guest to wrap his leftover food in a napkin and:
    A. Take it home.
    B. Give it to the poor.
    C. Give it to a priest.
    D. Return it to the kitchen.

11. While eating, it was considered polite to:
    A. Raise a finger up while drinking.
    B. Belch.
    C. Insult the food.
    D. Tip the slave.

12. In ancient Rome, it was considered a sin to eat the flesh of a(n):
    A. Eel.
    B. Woodpecker.
    C. White dove.
    D. Baboon.

13. Roman prophets would often tell the future and the feelings of the gods by:
    A. Examining a chicken's liver.
    B. Reading the Holy Scroll.
    C. Studying the stars.
    D. Examining bumps on a person's head.

14. In ancient Rome, the marriage ceremony began with a feast at the bride's home. The marriage celebration ended at the groom's home where he would:
    A. Carry the bride over the threshold.
    B. Live alone for one month.
    C. Receive money from the bride's father.
    D. Leave his bride and go out to celebrate.

15. Rich people kept a container in their kitchen filled with nuts and other delicacies that were used to fatten dormice. The fattened dormice were killed and:
    A. Sacrificed to the gods.
    B. Stuffed with sausage and eaten.
    C. Used to catch snakes.
    D. Were used in tossing contests.

Roman Customs and Superstitions Answers

1. **C. The left side of anything.** Some Romans would not even put on their left shoe first. The English word "sinister" is from a Latin word for "left."

2. **C. Sacrifice a pig.** Romans were very superstitious and felt that every spot on earth had a guardian spirit. In order to use that spot, farmers would have to appease that spirit by saying prayers and making a sacrifice.

3. **C. Vomit.** There was a room called a "vomitorium" that was used during a feast. People would eat as much as possible, go to the vomitorium, vomit, and return to eat some more. They might do this several times during the feast.

4. **C. Holly.**

5. **D. Genius.** Roman merchants and tradesmen often formed social clubs. Each month they would meet, enjoy a feast, and worship their patron spirit called their genius.

6. **A. With a crooked nose.**

7. **D. Go to the bathroom at the table.** In order to enjoy the feast without leaving the table, some guests would call a slave over and ask him to bring a pot, so that he could go to the bathroom without leaving the banquet.

8. **C. Impersonate the dead person.** An actor was hired to impersonate the dead relative, so the family could enjoy talking and interacting with the deceased one last time. They could also tell the deceased person how much he or she meant to them. Roman homes had a shrine where the family regularly went to pray. When a famous or wealthy person died, a mask was made of him and kept in the family shrine. The mask had skin made of wax and sported a wig.

9. **C. Reclined on a couch.** Romans usually did not sit at a table while they ate. Each guest lay on a couch and rested on the left elbow as he ate. Sitting while eating was appropriate for children and slaves. In the early part of the Roman Empire, women were required to sit while they ate. But as time passed, women as well as men reclined while they ate.

10. **A. Take it home.**

11. **B. Belch.**

12. **B. Woodpecker.**

13. **A. Examining a chicken's liver.** The prophets would often tell the future and the feelings of the gods by sacrificing a chicken and then examining its liver. Certain marks, bumps, or imperfections on the liver would tell the prophet the will of the gods. If the sacred chickens whose livers were used to tell the future were not eating, most Romans would not marry, travel, or plan a battle.

14. **A. Carry the bride over the threshold.** Since it was considered bad luck for a bride to touch the sill of a new home with her foot, the groom would carry the bride over the threshold. That tradition, begun by the Romans, is still followed today throughout the world. However, most marriages did not involve any kind of ceremony at all. There was no priest or government official that made the marriage legal. There were no formal records kept of the marriage. A couple was said to be married when they agreed to live together or when they referred to each other as husband and wife. Sometimes a marriage was recognized when the bride's family gave the husband a dowry. A couple became divorced by agreement or by leaving the home.

15. **B. Stuffed with sausage and eaten.**

46

Name: _____ Date: _____

Roman Emperors and Government

Circle the letter of the answer you believe correctly completes each statement.

1. The Emperor Heliogabalus of Rome had an odd hobby. He collected:
   A. Cobwebs.
   C. Autographs.
   B. Human heads.
   D. Philosophers.

2. When Nero became bored with someone, he would send them a note, suggesting they:
   A. Leave the city.
   C. Join the army.
   B. Kill themselves.
   D. Become more entertaining or leave.

3. When Claudius, who would someday become emperor, was young, Augustus ordered that he not be seen in public because:
   A. He was so ugly.
   C. It was feared that he would be killed.
   B. He was considered a god.
   D. His mother was a slave.

4. Gaius, whose nickname was Caligula, was an emperor. In order to frighten people, he:
   A. Practiced making faces in a mirror.
   C. Showed people a picture of his wife.
   B. Wore white makeup.
   D. Ordered them to be executed.

5. Gaius was given the nickname Caligula because:
   A. He struck terror in those he met.
   C. He had little feet.
   B. As a child, he could not say Gaius.
   D. He was named for his grand uncle.

6. A Roman counsel was a chief government administrator who commanded armies. Caligula once proposed that one of the counsels be:
   A. His wife.
   C. Cleopatra.
   B. His five-year-old son.
   D. His favorite horse.

7. Nero gave a present to Poppaea, his girlfriend. The present was:
   A. 300 slave girls.
   C. His wife's head.
   B. A personal bathhouse.
   D. Crete.

8. Romans had circuses that were much different than ours. Roman circuses were held in an arena and featured killing, fighting, and all sorts of other activities that caused death and bloodshed. While these activities occurred, Julius Caesar was often seen:
   A. Playing a lyre.
   C. Sleeping.
   B. Making bets.
   D. Writing letters.

9. When a messenger told Emperor Honorarius that "Rome is lost!", he became hysterical because:
   A. He was afraid he would be executed.
   C. All of his gold was in Rome.
   B. His family was in Rome at the time.
   D. "Rome" was the name of his pet chicken.

Name: _____ Date: _____

Roman Emperors and Government (cont.)

10. Which of the following did Nero **not** do?
    A. Fiddle or play while Rome burned   B. Act on stage
    C. Kill his mother   D. Kick his wife to death

11. The emperor Nero is described by writers of the day as someone who was very incompetent. Rather than being interested in running the empire, he was interested in drama, music, and writing. He loved to act in public. When he was acting:
    A. No one was permitted to watch.   B. The doors of the theater were locked.
    C. Only the aristocracy could watch.   D. He accompanied himself on the violin.

12. Nero went to Greece and participated in the Olympic Games. The Greeks had events for acting, chariot racing, singing, and playing the lute. When Nero participated in the chariot race, he was declared the winner in spite of the fact that:
    A. He finished last.   B. He did not finish the race.
    C. He fell out.   D. He used more horses than the others.

13. After Caesar became a dictator, he accomplished many things for Rome. He increased employment by constructing temples and other buildings. He established a huge library, which included only the best works written in Latin and Greek, and he made the library available to the public. One of his most important accomplishments was that he:
    A. Established a democracy.   B. Abolished slavery.
    C. Adopted Christianity.   D. Made a new calendar.

14. During the reign of Augustus, women:
    A. Paid no taxes.   B. Paid higher taxes than men.
    C. Paid lower taxes if they had children. D. Were taxed according to their height.

Roman Emperors and Government Answers

1. **A. Cobwebs.**
2. **B. Kill themselves.** Actually, the note said that the state would not mind if they killed themselves. A well-known philosopher named Seneca was given one of these notes; as a result, he stabbed himself with a sword.
3. **A. He was so ugly.** Claudius was a handsome man, but when he was young, he was so ugly that Augustus feared that people might laugh at him.
4. **A. Practiced making faces in a mirror.**
5. **C. He had little feet.** The Latin word *caligae* means "little boot." He had tiny feet and wore small soldiers' boots.
6. **D. His favorite horse.** This story is well-known, but some experts dispute it.
7. **C. His wife's head.** Nero not only had his wife murdered, but also had his mother put to death when she criticized his mistress, Poppaea Sabina. He later married Poppaea but later kicked her to death as well. There were many attempts to kill Nero. One man was exiled from Rome simply because he had the same name as one of Caesar's attempted assassins.
8. **D. Writing letters.** While most Romans found the circus exciting, those who saw it often might become bored. In fact, Julius Caesar was seen writing letters and making reports while the gladiators fought.
9. **D. "Rome" was the name of his pet chicken.** Honorarius, who had a pet chicken named "Rome," was hiding in his mansion from an invading army. A messenger came to him and said "Rome is lost!" Honorarius became hysterical until the messenger explained that when he said, "Rome was lost," he didn't mean the chicken, he meant the capital city of the empire.
10. **A. Fiddle or play while Rome burned.** There is a legend that Nero started a fire in Rome that destroyed most of the city and that he fiddled or played on his lyre while the fire burned. Nero was at Antium at the time and had nothing to do with the fire. Some say he blamed the Christians for the fire, but even this is in question. Nero rebuilt Rome and sheltered the homeless.
11. **B. The doors of the theater were locked.** When Nero was acting in public, the doors of the theater were locked and anyone who did not cheer for the emperor was hit by patrolling guards. During a revolt, Nero tried to leave and go to Egypt. The Senate declared him a public enemy and sentenced him to death. Instead, Nero committed suicide. Just before he died, he said, "What a showman the world is losing!"
12. **C. He fell out.** When Nero participated in the chariot race, he fell out but still won. He was so happy with his victory that he decreed that Greece would no longer have to pay tribute to Rome. "Tribute" was a tax.
13. **D. Made a new calendar.** The new calendar, called the Julian calendar, had 365 days each year for three years; then in the fourth year, it had an extra day. Caesar's calendar was used until 1582 in Europe, at which time Pope Gregory the XIII decreed that a new calendar (the Gregorian calendar) should be used.
14. **C. Paid lower taxes if they had children.** If a woman had three children, she was allowed to wear a special garment and was given freedom from her husband.

Name: _____ Date: _____

Roman Puzzle

Did you know that many of the words we use every day were borrowed from the Romans? Shown below are a number of definitions of these words. Fill in the spaces with the correct word that goes with the definitions. Then take the letters in the circles and put them in the spaces below the puzzle. The word that is spelled from these letters was something important to the Romans.

1. A stingy person
2. A powdery substance that hardens when mixed with water; it is an ingredient of concrete and mortar
3. A snake
4. The buildings and land of a school or university
5. To divide into two usually equal parts
6. A person who takes care of a collection of books
7. 1/36 of a yard
8. The smell or smoke given off by burning herbs

1. ☐☐☐☐ ◯
2. ☐☐☐ ◯☐☐
3. ☐☐☐ ◯☐☐☐
4. ☐☐☐☐ ◯☐
5. ◯☐☐☐☐☐
6. ◯☐☐☐☐☐☐☐
7. ◯☐☐☐
8. ☐☐◯☐☐☐

Answer: ___ ___ ___ ___ ___ ___ ___ ___

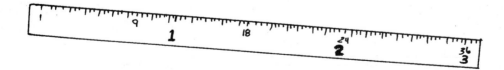

Name: _____ Date: _____

The Mongols

The Mongols were a nomadic people who lived on the elevated plateau in east central Asia. At about the beginning of the thirteenth century, Genghis Khan united many Mongolian tribes. This group of Mongols raided and destroyed many more highly developed countries and civilizations. For nearly two centuries, the Mongols dominated Asia and parts of Europe; they eventually created the largest empire the world had ever known. The Mongol Empire included the areas known today as Mongolia, China, Iraq, Iran, Afghanistan, Korea, and parts of Russia, Siberia, Turkey, Syria, Pakistan, India, Vietnam, and Cambodia. The Mongolians were able to accomplish this through the military genius of Genghis Khan and by the Mongol warriors who were among the most fierce fighters of all time.

Circle the letter of the answer you believe correctly completes each statement.

1. Which of the following was not a responsibility of a Mongol woman?
   A. Washing dishes
   B. Slitting throats
   C. Going into battle
   D. Preparing food

2. Mongols would never:
   A. Marry.
   B. Pray.
   C. Kill a horse.
   D. Take a bath.

3. Of the following, which is there no record of Mongols eating?
   A. Horses
   B. Lice
   C. Vegetables
   D. Human flesh

4. Mongols usually rode mares rather than stallions because:
   A. They could drink their milk.
   B. They were faster.
   C. They had more endurance.
   D. They were more obedient.

5. Mongols preferred to wear underwear made of what material?
   A. Deerskin
   B. Wool
   C. None
   D. Silk

6. Genghis Khan had _____ bodyguards.
   A. No
   B. 10
   C. 1,000
   D. 10,000

7. Mongols lived in:
   A. Mobile homes.
   B. Caves.
   C. Sod homes.
   D. Igloos.

8. When Genghis Khan conquered a city, he usually:
   A. Forbade worship.
   B. Killed priests.
   C. Gave tax exemptions to churches.
   D. Killed craftsmen.

Name: _____ Date: _____

The Mongols (cont.)

9. Every time Genghis Khan completed a successful battle, he:
   - A. Added a horse to his herd.
   - B. Branded a star in his horse.
   - C. Went on vacation.
   - D. Added a wife to his family.

10. If someone stepped on the tent flap of a person's house, they were:
    - A. Forced to apologize.
    - B. Put to death.
    - C. Made a slave.
    - D. Provided a new tent.

11. When a Mongol man died, his youngest son inherited:
    - A. Nothing.
    - B. His father's wives.
    - C. All of the household items.
    - D. His horses.

12. On one occasion, Kublai Khan ordered a group of _____ to attack and conquer a province.
    - A. Jugglers
    - B. Children
    - C. Women
    - D. Priests

13. A few minutes after the Mongols attacked a city, they often:
    - A. Stopped to pray.
    - B. Sang loud songs.
    - C. Lined up for instructions.
    - D. Retreated.

14. Mongols tenderized their dried meat by:
    - A. Putting it under their saddles.
    - B. Using Yeng's Meat Tenderizer.
    - C. Using salt.
    - D. Using a Flamenco dance.

15. Mongols were afraid of:
    - A. Nothing.
    - B. Mice.
    - C. Spiders.
    - D. Thunder.

16. Whenever a Mongol warrior went on a military conquest, he always brought along a:
    - A. Prayer book.
    - B. Sewing kit.
    - C. Compass.
    - D. Slave.

17. Which of the following weapons were **not** used by the Mongols in battle?
    - A. Rockets
    - B. Germ warfare
    - C. Grenades
    - D. Shields

18. The Khan would tell the future by reading:
    - A. Tea leaves.
    - B. Hairballs.
    - C. Sheep bones.
    - D. Nostradamus.

The Mongols Answers

1. **A. Washing dishes.** Mongol women did not generally participate in battles, unless the outcome of a fight was in doubt. Women had been trained from childhood, along with boys, to be excellent riders and archers. In addition, after a battle, one of the chores of a woman was to go to the battlefield and kill those who were wounded by slitting their throats. The Mongols never washed eating vessels or instruments.

2. **D. Take a bath.** Mongols refused to wash because they believed that very powerful spirits lived in the rivers and streams, and if they polluted the water by bathing in it, it would offend the spirits. For the same reason, they would never wash their clothes or eating vessels. They would wear their clothes until they literally fell apart. Sometimes, they would take off their clothes and beat them until most of the lice fell out, and then they would put them back on again.

3. **C. Vegetables.** Mongols ate just about anything they could find—dogs, foxes, horses, and wolves, but their diet consisted mainly of meat and a few dairy products. Almost every part of the animal was eaten. Even after the meat was cleaned off the bones, Mongols would break the bones open and eat the marrow before they threw the bone away. In all of the accounts of Mongol history, there is no reference to them eating vegetables or bread. While they did not generally consider lice a food, it was not uncommon for them to pop one in their mouths, if they found one crawling on them. Lice were a constant companion to the Mongols.

4. **A. They could drink their milk.** Mare's milk was a common food staple for Mongols. They would drink fresh mare's milk, or they dried it to take with them on journeys.

5. **D. Silk.** A Mongol's underwear was often made of fleece or wool, but he preferred to wear silk. The advantage of wearing silk underwear was not just comfort. Silk is an amazingly tough fabric. The Mongols had learned from the Chinese that if a soldier was hit by an arrow while wearing silk underwear, the arrowhead would not pierce the silk. The silk would wrap itself around the arrowhead. In order to remove the arrow from the warrior, all that was necessary was to pull the silk around the arrow, and it would come out with a minimum amount of damage.

6. **D. 10,000.** In order to be sure his commanders were loyal, Genghis Khan required that the commander's son or younger brother work for Genghis Khan as his guard or as a member of his household staff. If the commander was disloyal or acted in a cowardly manner,

The Mongols Answers (cont.)

the son or the younger brother would be executed. Many of these bodyguards traveled with their own families during a military campaign, so the house and court of Genghis Khan was as large as many cities.

7. **A. Mobile homes.** Mongols were a nomadic people, not staying in one place but moving often. They lived in homes called *gers*, that could be broken down and transported from one place to another. These were basically mobile homes that were almost round and had six sides. Each had a wooden frame covered with felt that was held in place by leather straps. The felt was treated with animal fat, making it weatherproof. The floor was made of planks covered with felt. There was a hearth where the family burned dried animal dung, which was used for cooking and heating. There was a hole in the roof for the smoke to escape and for light. The most important Mongols had separate *gers* for sleeping and cooking. Some Mongols even had separate *gers* for guests. Wealthy Mongols had a separate *ger* for each wife. Most *gers* were about 16 feet in diameter, but Genghis Khan's home could accommodate more than 100 people. Most Mongol homes could be taken apart and folded to make transporting them easier, but some were raised onto a heavy ox cart and moved without being taken apart. One European wrote that he once saw a cart with 22 oxen pulling one house. The driver was standing in the doorway of the house with the reins in his hands.

8. **C. Gave tax exemptions to churches.** Genghis Khan allowed all those he conquered to practice religion in any way they chose.

9. **D. Added a wife to his family.** When Genghis Khan died, he had 500 wives.

10. **B. Put to death.** There were felt idols next to the doorway of a Mongol's house. These idols represented the gods of good fortune and the gods of happiness. If someone accidentally stepped on the tent flap of a person's house, it was considered such an insult to these gods that the person who did it was put to death.

11. **B. His father's wives.** When a Mongol man died, all of his possessions, including his livestock and pasture land, was inherited by his sons. The oldest son was given the pasture land and animals farthest from the family's home base. The next oldest son was given the livestock and pasture land next to that of the oldest son, closer to the family's home base. This process would continue with each younger son inheriting livestock and land closer to the home base. The youngest son would be given the land the family considered the home base, as well as all of the father's wives, except his own mother. The youngest son would then become the husband of his stepmothers and the father of his stepbrothers and stepsisters.

12. **A. Jugglers.** Mongols were serious people but liked entertainment. There were dancers, acrobats, and even jugglers who entertained wealthy families. But even entertainers were expected to be warriors. On one occasion, Kublai Khan told the jugglers of his court to go and conquer a province. He said that he would give them a leader and troops to accompany them. The jugglers did what they were told and were successful in conquering the province.

The Mongols Answers (cont.)

13. **D. Retreated.** The Mongols used many ingenious battle tactics. On one occasion, they dammed up a river and then later broke the dam to flood the city. On another occasion when they were fighting on a frozen river, the Mongols scattered grit on their side of the ice and tied felt to their horses' hooves. While their enemies were slipping, sliding, and falling down, the Mongols kept their balance; they fought almost as effectively as if they were on land. However, their favorite tactic was the fake retreat. They would fight for awhile and then retreat on horseback. Their enemies would leave the safety of their city and follow, thinking they were winning. As they chased, the Mongols would twist in their saddles and shoot arrows at them. The Mongols had perfected their archery skills on horseback while hunting, so they would not only kill many of those pursuing them, but they would also kill many of their enemies' horses. When the remaining pursuers were completely exhausted, a fresh wave of Mongols, who had been hiding, would descend and massacre them.

14. **A. Putting it under their saddles.**

15. **D. Thunder.**

16. **B. Sewing kit.** The kit included an awl to pierce holes and sinews for stitching armor.

17. **D. Shields.** While Mongols used a shield on sentry duty, they did not use this shield in battle. The shield used on sentry duty was made of leather or wicker. They used catapults to send rocks and burning tar into the cities and onto walls and gates. When they went to war with China, they encountered rockets and grenades since the Chinese had invented gunpowder. The grenades were actually pods of clay packed with explosives and tossed by catapults or even by hand. Bamboo tube rockets were launched from a longbow. The Mongols adopted these weapons.

    In 1345, as the Mongols were laying siege to the city of Kaffa on the Black Sea, a strange sickness spread through the Mongol army, killing many and weakening their efforts. Instead of giving up and going home, the Mongols used their catapults to send corpses of those who had died of the disease over the city walls. When those inside the walls removed the Mongol corpses, they became infected and eventually infected others in the city. This is one of the first recorded cases of biological warfare. The disease was not contained in the city of Kaffa. It spread throughout the Mediterranean and Europe. The disease was known as the Black Death. It eventually killed one in every three Europeans.

18. **C. Sheep bones.** The Mongols believed that a shaman or the Khan could tell the future by reading sheep bones. If the tribe needed to make a decision about something important, the Khan had a slave bring him three shoulder blades from sheep. The Khan would hold the bones as he was thinking about the problem that was troubling the tribe. Then he would give the bones to the slave to be burned. When the bones turned black, they were returned to the Khan for inspection. If the fire split the bones lengthwise, in a straight line, the answer to his question was "yes." If, on the other hand, the bones cracked horizontally, then the answer was "no."

Name: _____ Date: _____

The Ancient Chinese

The Chinese civilization began along the Yellow River in north-central Asia about 2000 B.C. Until that time, there were various feudal lords who would wage war with each other. Even from the beginning, the Chinese had an appreciation of nature that could be found throughout Chinese life and culture. This appreciation of nature is found in Chinese agriculture, philosophy, religion, and social structure.

In the third century B.C., the ruler Qin Shihuang was so powerful that he conquered all of the other states. Since Qin is pronounced "Chin," the new nation became China. Qin's rule was very difficult for the Chinese people. There were many laws with harsh punishments and heavy taxes. After about 20 years, the people revolted, and the Qin Dynasty was replaced by a new dynasty called the Han dynasty; this dynasty is what many people refer to when they talk about the ancient Chinese civilization. The Han dynasty lasted for over 400 years.

Circle the letter of the answer you believe correctly completes each statement.

1. When a person died in Ancient China, two small bags were placed in the coffin containing:
   A. Money.
   B. Directions to the afterlife.
   C. Fingernails, toenails, and hair.
   D. Pictures of his ancestors.

2. The Great Wall of China was built for protection. Which of the following was **not** a name for the Great Wall in Ancient China?
   A. Great Wall
   B. The Longest Graveyard in the World
   C. Ten-Thousand-Mile-Long Wall
   D. The Silk Road

3. During the Qing dynasty (1644–1912), operas based on ancient Chinese folk stories and history became very popular. The actors would reveal the emotions of the characters by exaggerated gestures. If an actor was surprised, he might:
   A. Stomp loudly.
   B. Do a number of back flips.
   C. Belch.
   D. Run and hide.

4. If a husband and wife were in public, the wife was required to:
   A. Be completely covered.
   B. Wear a dress of white silk.
   C. Be chained to his wrist.
   D. Walk ten paces behind her husband.

5. In ancient China, this was considered a sign of beauty:
   A. A bald head
   B. Blue eyes
   C. Small feet
   D. Long toenails

6. Most farmers had some livestock on their farms. Which of the following animals were **not** raised for food in these times?
   A. Cows
   B. Sheep
   C. Pigs
   D. Dogs

Name: _____ Date: _____

The Ancient Chinese (cont.)

7. At a funeral when the lid of the coffin was closed, mourners would:
   A. Hurl themselves on the coffin.
   B. Take a few steps backward.
   C. Shout, "Farewell, friend."
   D. Clap in unison.

8. In China during the sixteenth and seventeenth centuries, which of the following would a person **not** consider using if he wanted to kill someone?
   A. Knife
   B. Poison
   C. Tiger's claws
   D. Tiger's whiskers

9. In ancient China, towns were often arranged in:
   A. The shapes of animals.
   B. Squares.
   C. Circles.
   D. Pentagons.

10. Although a woman could not divorce her husband, she could contest a divorce if she met one of three conditions. Which of the following is **not** one of the conditions?
    A. She had no relatives to take her.
    B. She had given birth to a male child.
    C. He had become wealthy while he was married.
    D. She had mourned the death of one of her husband's parents for three years.

11. Part of Korea's taxes were paid to China in:
    A. Tiger skins.
    B. Fish skins.
    C. Albino eels.
    D. Kites.

12. Where the Emperor lived, what he wore, and what he ate depended on:
    A. His desires.
    B. His religious advisors.
    C. What was available.
    D. The season of the year.

13. During the Han Dynasty, wealthy Chinese families often had their own:
    A. Wall for protection.
    B. Army.
    C. Five-piece orchestra.
    D. Philosopher.

14. At the end of the growing season, the Chinese had a festival to honor the spirits who protected the season's crops from predators and natural disasters. They honored:
    A. Tigers and cats.
    B. Rain and sun.
    C. Yin and Yang.
    D. Earth, wind, and fire.

15. When a Chinese mother was about to have a baby, the parents of the mother-to-be would send her presents:
    A. To ensure a male child.
    B. To hasten the birth.
    C. For the privilege of naming the child.
    D. As part of the mother's dowry.

16. Chinese people felt that this prevented a dead body from decaying:
    A. Dry ice
    B. Oil of retina
    C. Rice wine
    D. Jade

Name: _____ Date: _____

The Ancient Chinese (cont.)

17. Chinese fathers named their children:
    A. Three months before they were born.   B. When they were born.
    C. Three months after they were born.   D. When they married.

18. When a Chinese boy became 20 years of age, his schooling was complete, and he was considered an adult. To mark this occasion, there was a ceremony where he was given:
    A. A bride.   B. A shield and a spear.
    C. Three hats.   D. Forty acres and a mule.

19. In ancient China, poor people were able to survive by selling:
    A. Apples.   B. Their mother-in-law.
    C. Themselves into slavery.   D. Their children.

20. Divorce was allowed under certain conditions in ancient China. Which of the following was **not** a reason for a Chinese man to divorce his wife?
    A. Not bearing children   B. Talking too much
    C. Becoming old   D. Disobedience to in-laws

21. In the second century A.D., the Chinese built an astronomical clock. It was 39 feet tall and had almost 200 wooden puppets that beat drums and made musical sounds. It was five stories high and was powered by:
    A. Water.   B. Slaves.
    C. Horses.   D. The tide.

22. Changan, the capital city, was laid out in the same pattern as:
    A. A dragon.   B. The Big Dipper.
    C. Rome.   D. The Forbidden City.

23. In early China, the weather report was given by:
    A. Watching silkworms.   B. Watching the moon.
    C. Reading tea leaves.   D. Reading animal bones.

24. During the Han dynasty (202 B.C.–A.D. 220), there were books written on all but one of the following. Which one?
    A. Etiquette   B. Farming
    C. Cooking   D. Tiger hunting

25. The ancient Chinese read many different signs in nature in order to tell the future. Halos around the moon, rainbows, and even meteor showers were all signs of future events. Another way to tell the future was by:
    A. Gazing into a ball of jade.   B. Reading palms.
    C. Rolling dice.   D. Throwing sticks down on the ground.

58

The Ancient Chinese Answers

1. **C. Fingernails, toenails, and hair.** Clippings from their hair and nails were collected throughout their life; when they died, these clippings were put into bags and placed next to the body, so when the dead person went into the next world, he would be complete.

2. **D. The Silk Road.** During the Han dynasty, the Wall was called the "Ten-Thousand-Mile-Long Wall." Those building the Great Wall worked under very harsh conditions. In the winter, it was cold; in the summer, it was very hot. Since many of those working on the wall were convicts, the Emperor did not care if these people lived or died. Many were literally worked to death and were buried next to the wall. The wall became known as the "Longest Graveyard in the World." The Silk Road was an ancient trade route that linked China with the West. The Silk Road was a commercial link between East and West and a link that spread the political, social, artistic, and religious customs of the Chinese to the West.

3. **B. Do a number of back flips.** If he was angry, he might twirl around the stage like a tornado.

4. **D. Walk ten paces behind her husband.** The woman had to obey her husband without question. He could beat her or divorce her if he wanted to. A wife could never divorce her husband.

5. **C. Small feet.** Mothers would tightly wrap their daughters' feet with cloth, so the feet could not grow. This practice is called *foot-binding*. Foot-binding was first begun with dancers in the palace to make their feet smaller and more feminine. It was the goal to make the feet as small as possible. Five-inch feet were considered the ideal at one time; gradually, that number was lowered to three inches. Obviously, a young woman whose feet had been bound to reach only three inches would be deformed. Her toes would be curled under her feet, and her instep would be broken. Consequently, she could not walk very well. Another purpose of foot-binding was to show a wife's submission to her husband.

6. **A. Cows.** The diet of the ancient Chinese consisted mainly of grain, beans, and other vegetables which they supplemented with small amounts of meat from animals they kept. Their livestock consisted of pigs, chickens, ducks, sheep, and dogs. Some people owned cattle, but they were used mainly to pull carts and plows. They did not raise cattle because cattle over-grazed the land and caused soil erosion; this would make it difficult for future crops to grow. They did not drink the milk of cattle because they considered milk a drink of barbarians.

The Ancient Chinese Answers (cont.)

7. **B. Take a few steps backward.** It was considered bad luck if a person's shadow was caught in the coffin as it was closing.

8. **C. Tiger's claws.** Finely-chopped tiger's whiskers placed in food is deadly. The whiskers get caught in the digestive tract and cause sores and infections.

9. **A. The shapes of animals.** In ancient China, towns were often arranged in patterns, so if they were seen from the air, the town would resemble an animal or a symbolic design. Some were arranged to resemble snakes, stars, sunbursts, and dragons.

10. **B. She had given birth to a male child.**

11. **B. Fish skins.** Fish skins were used to make shoes for Kublai Khan, who had gout. Gout is an arthritic disease that causes pain, tenderness, and swelling around the joints and tendons.

12. **D. The season of the year.** The Chinese believed that to live in harmony with nature, they had to respect the cycles of the seasons and the directions of north, south, east, and west. The Emperor would wear green and live in the Eastern Pavilion in the spring. In summer, he would wear red and live in the Southern Pavilion. In autumn, he would wear white and reside in the Western Pavilion. In winter, he would move to the Northern Pavilion and would wear black. His meals would vary from season to season as well. In autumn, for example, one of his main meals was dog meat.

13. **C. Five-piece orchestra.** Wealthy Chinese families had their own performers to entertain them. Some even had five-piece orchestras. The instruments were percussion instruments, string, and wind instruments.

14. **A. Tigers and cats.** Tigers killed wild boars that invaded the fields, and cats killed the rats that ate the grain. Both adults and children costumed themselves as cats and tigers during the celebration.

15. **B. To hasten the birth.** Following the birth, the mother would also receive many gifts. On a child's first birthday, different objects were placed around him. The first item he chose indicated the occupation the child would eventually choose.

16. **D. Jade.** Small pieces of jade were put under the tongue and over the eyes of the deceased.

17. **C. Three months after they were born.** Before three months, the child was not considered fit to be in the presence of the father. When the father would tell the child his name, he would say it in a very childlike voice so as not to frighten the child. When both boys and girls became adults, they were involved in a ceremony where they would receive a new name. Their new names would be the names that would be used in public so their original name would not be revealed. The point of the new names was to show respect for adults and to give them privacy by not using their original name in public. A boy's name might also be changed later in life if he were involved in some important event. Important people sometimes even received a new name after they were dead.

18. **C. Three hats.** The ceremony, which was an announcement that the young man was no longer a boy but an adult, was called the Capping Ceremony. At this ceremony, the young man would change his hairstyle from that of a boy to the hairstyle of a man. The

The Ancient Chinese Answers (cont.)

boy's hairstyle was two horns on the side of the head. A man's hairstyle was a coil on top of the head. This was called the Capping Ceremony because several different caps or hats were put on the young man. Since he was no longer a boy, he could no longer go out in public without a hat on his head; therefore, he was given a plain cloth hat. He was then given another hat that represented his willingness to fight for his people. He was given still another hat to be used to lead the rituals that honored his ancestors. After the ceremony, the boy was considered a man and was able to become a warrior, get married, and become a civil servant if he were able to pass an exam. He was also old enough to conduct a worship service for his ancestors.

When a girl reached an age where she could be married, she also went through a ceremony, but it was not as elaborate as the Capping Ceremony for boys. She did not receive caps, but she received a hairpin. As a child, she wore her hair braided in a cross in the middle of her head. The hairpin she received at her ceremony was to change her hairstyle so her hair could be worn on top of her head.

19. **D. Their children.** This practice was more common when there was famine or drought. A father might sell his older daughter as a slave to a wealthy family. Occasionally, after the famine was over and if the family could afford it, the family was permitted to buy the daughter back. Girls who were too young to be sold were sometimes given away, sent to monasteries, or killed.

20. **C. Becoming old.** Other grounds for divorcing a woman were adultery, theft, disobediency to the husband or her husband's parents, jealousy, and incurable disease. If they did not have any children, it was assumed that the wife was at fault. Having male children was important to Chinese society; without a male heir, the family would not survive. There would not be anyone to honor and sacrifice for their dead ancestors. If she were chronically sick or if she were disobedient, she might not be able to prepare the sacrifices for her husband's ancestors.

21. **A. Water.**

22. **B. The Big Dipper.** The city of Changan, the capital city, was laid out in the same pattern as the stars in the constellation we call the Big Dipper.

23. **D. Reading animal bones.** Advisers to the king would use a heated rod on a prepared animal bone to make cracks. The cracks would then be interpreted and would tell them all sorts of things, including what the weather would be like. In early China, historical records were written on ox bones and turtle shells.

24. **D. Tiger hunting.** During the Han dynasty there was a book of etiquette entitled, *Chinese Civilization and Society: A Source Book.* This book gave specific instructions in the ways an average citizen was expected to act in society.

25. **D. Throwing sticks down on the ground.** They thought that the pattern the sticks made when they landed on the ground foretold the future.

Name: _____ Date: _____

Scrambled Headlines From the Ancient World

Shown below are several headlines that could have appeared in the Ancient World if there had been newspapers. The only problem is that they are mixed up. Each headline has been broken into three parts. Each part is shown in one of three columns. Columns two and three have been scrambled. Begin with the name in the first column, and then find one phrase from the second column and one phrase from the third column to complete each headline. Write the completed headlines on the form on the following page. You may mark off the phrases as you use them. The first headline is given as an example.

1. ~~Antony and Cleopatra~~   buries Pompeii,   as a tomb of King Cheops

2. The Great Pyramid   whom many called the Messiah,   is adopted by the Greeks

3. The Buddha,   is assassinated by Brutus   no building remains

4. Julius Caesar   ~~commit suicide~~   for his beautiful wife

5. Hammurabi   invented by the Phoenicians,   is crucified for heresy

6. A colossal Sphinx   builds Great Wall   in Babylon to protect the weak

7. Vesuvius erupts,   Ramses II, dies   a pharaoh's tomb from demons

8. Hannibal   creates hanging gardens   after ruling for 67 years

9. China   develops a code of laws   is developed to honor the gods

10. Jesus Christ,   the father of medicine,   drinks hemlock

11. Olympic Games,   is erected in Egypt   searches for the truth

12. Socrates,   known as the enlightened one,   to protect itself from barbarians

13. The alphabet,   condemned to death,   to invade Italy

14. King Nebuchadnezzar   a sports festival,   develops oath for doctors

15. Egypt's greatest pharaoh,   was built to protect   to prevent him from becoming king

16. Hippocrates,   crosses Alps on elephants   ~~after fleeing from Egypt~~

Name: _____ Date: _____

Scrambled Headlines From the Ancient World

Write the completed headlines from page 62 on the lines below. The first one has been done for you.

1. *Antony and Cleopatra commit suicide after fleeing from Egypt* _____

2. _____

3. _____

4. _____

5. _____

6. _____

7. _____

8. _____

9. _____

10. _____

11. _____

12. _____

13. _____

14. _____

15. _____

16. _____

Name: _____ Date: _____

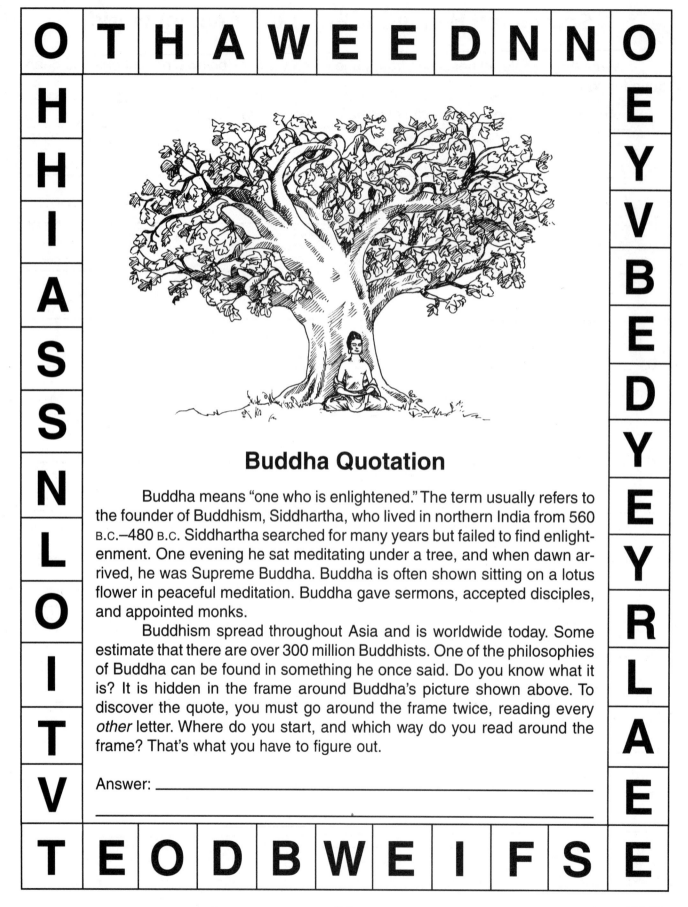

Buddha Quotation

Buddha means "one who is enlightened." The term usually refers to the founder of Buddhism, Siddhartha, who lived in northern India from 560 B.C.–480 B.C. Siddhartha searched for many years but failed to find enlightenment. One evening he sat meditating under a tree, and when dawn arrived, he was Supreme Buddha. Buddha is often shown sitting on a lotus flower in peaceful meditation. Buddha gave sermons, accepted disciples, and appointed monks.

Buddhism spread throughout Asia and is worldwide today. Some estimate that there are over 300 million Buddhists. One of the philosophies of Buddha can be found in something he once said. Do you know what it is? It is hidden in the frame around Buddha's picture shown above. To discover the quote, you must go around the frame twice, reading every *other* letter. Where do you start, and which way do you read around the frame? That's what you have to figure out.

Answer: _____

_____

Name: ______________________ Date: ______________________

E M T D S N E A L S G

I P L T E T S A B J E O

U N O I H S T A A H F T O

G U I R N N S E W Y I

Confucius Quotation

Confucius was a wise Chinese man who lived from 551 B.C.–479 B.C. He was best known as a teacher. One of the basic doctrines Confucius taught was that we should treat everyone with kindness.

The sayings of Confucius were assembled into a book. One of his sayings can be found hidden in the frame around the picture of Confucius shown above. To discover the saying, you must go around the frame twice, reading every *other* letter. Where do you start, and which way do you read around the frame? That's what you have to figure out.

Answer: ____

____

Name: _____ Date: _____

Vikings

The Vikings, who lived in Scandinavia between 800 and 1100, left their homes to trade and raid along the Baltic, North, and Irish Seas and along the rivers of Eastern and Western Europe. The Vikings were farmers who kept livestock and lived near the sea so they could fish. The Vikings prospered with their trade, and when land became scarce in Scandinavia, they traveled along the coasts of Western Europe, seeking farmland and plunder. They not only raided villages and churches, they settled and intermingled with those they invaded.

Circle the letter of the answer you believe correctly completes each statement.

1. Vikings thought that those who died in battle went to a heavenly hall in Valhalla where they spent their days:
A. Feasting.
B. Sleeping.
C. Fighting.
D. Working.

2. According to a Viking legend, in the beginning, there was one man and one woman who came from:
A. The marriage of two gods.
B. The tears of a blue heron.
C. Toledo.
D. The sweat of a giant's armpit.

3. A Viking legend said that the clouds in the sky were really:
A. The brains of dead giants.
B. Ice mountains.
C. The souls of the dead.
D. The breath of the gods.

4. A Viking saga indicated that the sky was held up by:
A. Elephants.
B. A giant.
C. Huge turtles.
D. Four dwarfs.

5. Vikings believed that if they had a peaceful death, they went directly to:
A. Heaven.
B. Hel.
C. To a new body.
D. Amsterdam.

6. Vikings believed that Hel was:
A. Very hot.
B. Very cold.
C. A paradise.
D. A party that would last through eternity.

7. Sometimes, when a Viking died in a foreign land far from home, his body was:
A. Wrapped in bearskin.
B. Painted.
C. Buried upside-down.
D. Boiled.

8. A Viking named Sigurd had an unusual death. He was killed:
A. By a three-day-old child.
B. By a dead man.
C. By a fly.
D. By a song.

Name: _____ Date: _____

Vikings (cont.)

9. When the Vikings went into a battle, some would wear shirts made of interlocking iron rings, while others wore padded leather jackets. The most fierce fighters would wear:
    A. A snarl.
    B. An iron loincloth.
    C. A small piece of animal skin.
    D. A silk tunic.

10. Which of the following was not the name of a Viking?
    A. Keith Flatnose
    B. Harold Bluetooth
    C. Olaf the Peacock
    D. Goody Two-Shoes

11. When a Viking man arrived in a new country, he was free to claim land. The amount he could claim depended on how much land he walked around in one day while carrying a flaming torch. Viking women could also claim land, but a woman could only claim as much land as she could walk around in one day:
    A. Leading a two-year-old cow.
    B. Walking backwards.
    C. Walking blindfolded.
    D. Carrying her child.

12. What well-known nursery rhyme was actually based on a Viking raid?
    A. Mary Had a Little Lamb
    B. Ring-a-Ring O' Roses
    C. London Bridge Is Falling Down
    D. Row, Row, Row Your Boat

13. After the Vikings had a steam bath, they would:
    A. Walk on hot stones.
    B. Spray themselves with cold water.
    C. Rub themselves with salt.
    D. Run outside and roll in the snow.

14. Vikings made ice skates to cross frozen rivers. The skates were made of bones and were called:
    A. Ice-legs.
    B. Ice skates.
    C. People movers.
    D. Sliders.

15. Of a Viking slave and a freeman, a slave was buried:
    A. Closer to the church.
    B. Farther from the church.
    C. Only after his master died.
    D. In a foreign country.

16. Slaves, who were called thralls, were known by some very colorful names. Which of the following was not recorded as a slave's name?
    A. Bundle of rags
    B. Horsefly
    C. Ashen face
    D. Squeezebox

17. When a blacksmith tempers metal, he heats it to a very high temperature, and then quickly cools it by dipping it in water. The Vikings learned this technique for hardening their swords; however, sometimes instead of using water, they would cool the heated sword by dipping it in:
    A. Beer.
    B. Blood.
    C. Wine.
    D. Holy water.

67

Vikings Answers

1. **C. Fighting.** Fighting was an important part of a Viking's life. Their idea of Valhalla was a place where those who had died in battle would spend their days fighting and their nights feasting. If they happened to die in one of these battles, they came back to life and were able to fight again the next day.

2. **D. The sweat of a giant's armpit.**

3. **A. The brains of dead giants.**

4. **D. Four dwarfs.** The dwarfs' names were North, South, East, and West.

5. **B Hel.** The Vikings believed that if they died in battle, they went directly to Valhalla. If, however, they had a peaceful death, they went directly to Hel.

6. **B. Very cold.**

7. **D. Boiled.** Their bodies were boiled until there were just enough bones left to be carried home in a box.

8. **B. By a dead man.** Here's what happened. Sigurd killed a man in battle and as was the custom, he cut off the man's head and put it on his saddle. A tooth from the head of the dead man scratched Sigurd's leg; as a result, the leg became infected, and it killed him.

9. **C. A small piece of animal skin.** The fighters were called *berserkers*, which means "bear shirt." This is where the word *berserk* comes from. *Berserkers* would fight savagely believing the animal skin would give them the courage and strength of the animal whose skin they were wearing.

10. **D. Goody Two-Shoes.** Some Vikings were named after gods or animals. However, many of the Viking names we know today were really nicknames. Here are some other Viking names: Olaf the Stout, Harald Redbeard, Harold Bluetooth, Erik Blood-Axe and Asgot the Clumsy.

11. **A. Leading a two-year-old cow.** The Vikings settled in many different countries. Some of the countries were uninhabited when they settled, but others were gained by conquest.

12. **C. London Bridge Is Falling Down.** Every English-speaking child has heard and has sung the song "London Bridge Is Falling Down." What most people do not know, however, is that this song was written about a Viking attack on London. A Viking named Olaf attacked London, and as he did, he was fired upon by English soldiers who were on London Bridge. The soldiers' arrows were killing Vikings and infuriatied Olaf so much that he attached ropes to the base of London Bridge and the other ends of the ropes to his ships. Then the Vikings rowed as fast as they could, causing London Bridge to begin to fall down.

13. **D. Run outside and roll in the snow.** Vikings had bathhouses similar to our saunas. In these bathhouses, water was poured over hot stones, causing steam to rise. People would sit in these bathhouses, become very warm, and sweat. Then they would whip themselves with twigs or branches from a tree or shrub and run outside and roll in the snow.

Vikings Answers (cont.)

14. **A. Ice-legs.** In order to propel themselves across the frozen water, they would push themselves with poles. This was similar to the way people ski today.

15. **B. Farther from the church.** There were several different classes in the Viking culture,
which was important in determining where a person was buried. Freemen, along with
their wives and children, were buried closest to the church. Thralls, who were slaves,
were buried farther from the church. Even farther away from the thralls were the drowned
bodies of people found along the shore. If the corpse had a Norwegian hairstyle, it was
buried farthest away from the church. If it did not have the Norwegian hairstyle, it was
not buried in the church graveyard.

16. **D   Squeezebox.** Here are some other slave's names. Stinking, Shouter, Blob-nose, Oaf,
Servant, Fat Thighs, Noisy, Cattleman, and Shelter.

17. **B. Blood.**

Viking Puzzle

Shown below are a number of scrambled words we use today that were originally Viking words. Unscramble them and put them in the spaces beside each scrambled word. Then place the letter in each circle on the lines below. The letters will spell out a word that is very important to the Vikings.

KSY   (S) K Y

RACSE   ◯ __ __ __ __

EXAL   ◯ __ __ __

NFIEK   __ ◯ __ __ __

DOD   __ __ ◯

SINK   __ __ ◯ __

NAWD   __ __ ◯ __

RCWAL   __ __ ◯ __ __

VIEG   __ __ ◯ __

TAIB   __ __ ◯ __

TRAF   __ ◯ __ __

Answer: S__ __ __ __ __ __ __ __ __ __ __

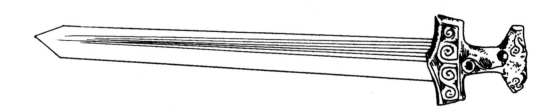

Name: _____   Date: _____

Runes

Runes are the letters of an ancient Germanic alphabet used from about 100 B.C. to A.D. 1700. The runic alphabet was used in Scandinavia, Northern Europe, the British Isles, and Iceland. Runes were used to record inscriptions, charms, and magic on stone, wood, metal, or bone. Runic inscriptions have even been discovered in North America, which gives support to the belief that Vikings came to the Americas before Columbus. Use the Rune below to decode the missing words in the following message.

| A | B | C | D | E | F | G | H | I | K | L | M | N | O | P | Q | R | S | T | UVW | X | Y | Z |

(1) _____ is not only a god of (2) _____ and (3) _____, he is also the god of (4) _____ and (5) _____. It is written that he hung for nine days on the (6) _____ (7) _____, pierced by his (8) _____. While there, he learned nine powerful (9) _____ and eighteen (10) _____. His (11) _____ is in his hall in (12) _____. From this throne, he can see everything that is happening in the (13) nine _____. He also lives in (14) _____, where the slain (15) _____ are taken.

1. _____   2. _____   3. _____   4. _____

5. _____   6. _____   7. _____

8. _____   9. _____   10. _____

11. _____   12. _____   13. _____

14. _____   15. _____

Name: _____ Date: _____

Middle Ages

The Middle Ages is generally considered to be the period between the end of the Roman Empire and the beginning of the Renaissance. This roughly translates from the years 500 to 1500. The sacking of Rome by the Visigoths and the deposition of Romulus Augustulus as Western emperor in 476 are two events that often are given as the end of Ancient Civilization. The beginning of the Modern Age is sometimes considered 1453 with the fall of Constantinople to the Turks.

Circle the letter of the answer you believe correctly completes each statement.

1. During the Middle Ages, those who were insane were:
   A. Worshipped.
   C. Executed.
   B. Tied in church.
   D. Excommunicated.

2. Which of the following were admitted to a hospital during the Middle Ages?
   A. Those who were wounded
   C. The blind
   B. Those who were crippled
   D. Those who were pregnant

3. Most people had their teeth pulled at:
   A. Home by traveling dentists.
   C. Fairs by barbers.
   B. Church.
   D. The butcher shop.

4. Manners in the Middle Ages dictated that people should always _____ before taking a drink from a cup.
   A. Say a prayer
   C. Make a toast
   B. Wipe their mouths
   D. Salute the host

5. The Easter celebration lasted approximately:
   A. One day.
   C. Twelve days.
   B. One week.
   D. 120 days.

6. During the Middle Ages, the bodies of dead saints were:
   A. Broken up and treasured.
   C. Buried under church altars.
   B. Worshipped.
   D. Dried and displayed.

7. A common Scottish dish was haggis. Haggis was a stuffed:
   A. Snake.
   C. Head of lamb.
   B. Sheep's stomach.
   D. Pigeon.

8. At this time, tooth decay was thought to be caused by:
   A. Evil spirits.
   C. Worms.
   B. The Tooth Fairy.
   D. Rancid food.

Name: _____ Date: _____

Middle Ages (cont.)

9. The Hundred Years' War lasted:
   A. 76 years.
   B. 100 years.
   C. 116 years.
   D. 127 years.

10. When a person from the lower classes went to town, they needed to be concerned that they were not picked up by the:
    A. Tax collector.
    B. Fashion police.
    C. Army recruiter.
    D. Priest patrol.

11. Which of the following medical procedures was **not** used in the Middle Ages?
    A. Cosmetic surgery
    B. Brain surgery
    C. Use of anesthesia
    D. Inoculation for smallpox

12. A tablecloth, when placed on a table, had one side longer than the other. The long side was used:
    A. To keep the diners warm.
    B. To cover an unmarried woman.
    C. As a napkin.
    D. Prevent drafts.

13. When a child was being born, everything in the house:
    A. Was sterilized.
    B. Was blessed.
    C. That was closed was opened.
    D. Covered with drapes.

14. After a child was born, he or she was:
    A. Rubbed with salt.
    B. Bathed in spring water.
    C. Bathed in beer.
    D. Handed to the father.

15. Heavy spices were often used in food:
    A. To provide warmth on cold nights.
    B. Because the food was often spoiled.
    C. For religious reasons.
    D. To impress guests.

16. Which of the following birds were not eaten at meals?
    A. Peacocks
    B. Vultures
    C. Turkeys
    D. Swans

17. During the fourteenth and fifteenth centuries, the church had a rule against:
    A. Surgery.
    B. Women doctors.
    C. Massage therapy.
    D. Jewish doctors.

18. Ague, which was a fever, was treated by:
    A. Drinking beer.
    B. Standing in the rain.
    C. Swallowing live goldfish.
    D. Swallowing a raisin with a spider in it.

Name: _____ Date: _____

Middle Ages (cont.)

19. Baldness was treated by rubbing the bald head with:
    A. Bear fat.
    B. Holy water.
    C. Goose droppings.
    D. Tree sap.

20. The treatment for a toothache was to:
    A. Eat a jalapeno pepper.
    B. Touch a dead man's tooth.
    C. Rub the tooth with bone marrow.
    D. Eat a ground-up horse's tooth.

21. A woman carried an acorn because she thought it would:
    A. Protect her from lightning.
    B. Keep away wild animals.
    C. Give her good luck.
    D. Keep her from aging.

22. At dinner, the meal would be announced by a crier, and when a guest entered, the lord of the house would:
    A. Kiss the guest.
    B. Applaud the guest.
    C. Belch loudly.
    D. Hand the guest his plate and fork.

23. When the guests and hosts were standing by the dinner table, they could not sit down until they:
    A. Toasted the host.
    B. Washed their hands.
    C. Prayed.
    D. Sang a song of thanksgiving.

24. People's food in the Middle Ages was placed on "trenchers." Trenchers were:
    A. Cabbage leaves.
    B. Thick slices of bread.
    C. Platters.
    D. China plates.

25. Which of the following hair preparations or tools were **not** used in the Middle Ages?
    A. Hairpins
    B. Curling irons
    C. Hair dye
    D. Hair dryers

26. The celebration that concluded The Twelve Days of Christmas was called Twelfth Night. On the twelfth night, a couple was chosen that were named the King and Queen of:
    A. Winterfest.
    B. The Bean.
    C. Christmas.
    D. Snow.

27. After supper during the Twelve Days of Christmas celebration, the people would gather to drink a toast to:
    A. Father Christmas.
    B. The king.
    C. The bunnies of the forest.
    D. The trees.

28. Smallpox was treated by:
    A. Eating chicken soup.
    B. Wrapping the victim in red cloth.
    C. Sweating in a sauna.
    D. Drinking sour milk.

Middle Ages Answers

1. **B. Tied in church.** Those who were insane were considered to be possessed by demons or the devil, and the church performed exorcisms to rid them of these demons. Crosses were shaved into their heads. Some would be tied in church so they could hear the mass and rid themselves of the demons.

2. **A. Those who were wounded.** Hospitals were set up by the church and were one of the most important innovations of the Middle Ages. Hospitals were for the wounded and incurably sick people. Those who were crippled, blind, pregnant, or had the plague or leprosy were not admitted to the hospital.

3. **C. Fairs by barbers.** Most people had their teeth pulled by barbers who set up booths at fairs and markets, although very poor peasants often pulled their own teeth. There were dentists during the Middle Ages, but only the wealthy could afford them. The wealthy had dentists remove decay and fill cavities with ground bone. By the fifteenth century, gold fillings were used. Loose teeth were repaired and strengthened by using metal binders. False teeth were made of oxen bone and other materials.

4. **B. Wipe their mouths.** Cups were usually shared by two different people. Other table manners included not spitting across a table, not wiping their mouths on their sleeves, not poking their fingers in eggs, and not gnawing on bones with their teeth. They were also not to belch, lean over the food, or put their elbows on the table.

5. **D. 120 days.** During Lent, which started on Ash Wednesday and ended on Easter Day, no marriages could take place, and fasting was expected.

6. **A. Broken up and treasured.** Although the Roman Church criticized the practice, Christians from the East and pagans would break up the bodies of dead saints to use as relics. In the middle of the fourth century, the West began to do the same. Relics were sought-after because it reminded people of the faith and good deeds of the saints. Also, their bodies were considered to be purified and blessed souls. Not only the bodies, but also personal belongings, such as clothing and objects that belonged to the saints, were revered. Most Christians, even those who were poor, tried to buy at least one relic.

7. **B. Sheep's stomach.** It was stuffed with onions, liver, oatmeal, beef, and heart. Here is a recipe for haggis. A sheep's stomach should be soaked in salted water for about 12 hours. Then turn the rough side out, wash the small bag, hang the windpipe over the edge of the pot, cover the stomach with water and boil for an hour or two. Then cut off the pipe and gristle, chop the heart, and halve the liver and add to chopped onions, oatmeal, and garlic. Moisten these ingredients with broth. Put the mixture inside the bag and sew it closed. Boil the stomach for about three hours and cut a small hole in the bag when it begins to swell. Another popular dish in England was entrayale. This consisted of a sheep's stomach stuffed with vegetables, eggs, cheese, bread, and pork. And you thought cafeteria food was gross!

8. **C. Worms.**

9. **C. 116 years** (1337–1453).

10. **B. Fashion police.** Wealth and station in life were apparent by the way people dressed. Certain styles of clothing and fabrics could only be used by the upper classes. There were actually "fashion police" who would walk the streets checking clothing to be sure that no one was dressing above his or her class.

Middle Ages Answers (cont.)

11. **D. Inoculation for smallpox.** Edward Jenner, an English physician, discovered inoculation for smallpox in 1798. However, during the fifteenth century, successful cosmetic surgery was performed using skin grafts and bones to reconstruct noses, ears, lips, and other parts of the body. Anesthesia in the Middle Ages consisted of a sponge soaked with opium and other herbs. It was placed over a patient's nose and mouth before a medical procedure in order to render him or her unconscious.

12. **C. As a napkin.** The tablecloth was changed between courses.

13. **C. That was closed was opened.** Doors were opened, and lids were taken off pots. Even ropes were untied. It was believed that this would help ease the mother's pain. Doctors did not take care of pregnant women. When a woman was about to have a baby, a midwife would be called to help deliver the child.

14. **A. Rubbed with salt.** Then his mouth would be cleaned with honey.

15. **B. Because the food was often spoiled.** Heavy spices disguised spoiled and rotten food.

16. **C. Turkeys.** Turkeys were not native to Europe. In 1520, turkeys were brought to England from Mexico. While you might think that most meals in the Middle Ages were simple, you would be wrong. Many were elaborate. Swans were sometimes cooked with all their feathers still on their body. The heads of animals such as pigs and other animals were left on as they were cooked, or the carcass may have been cooked separately, and then the heads sewn back on afterwards.

17. **A. Surgery.** During the Middle Ages, the church did not approve of medical studies since it was believed that illness was considered a punishment from God for sinning. Those who were ill often took pilgrimages to holy places in the hope of recovery. Some medical students defied the church and studied medicine by dissecting pigs and executed convicts. Most surgeries were performed by a barber/surgeon. Most of the doctors during the Middle Ages were men. Jewish doctors were considered the best because they could speak many languages, including Greek and Arabic. However, ordinary, everyday medicine was often performed by women. They used herbs, salves, and other folk remedies that had been passed down from generation to generation. They also used massage as a therapy. There were some women doctors who specialized in certain kinds of illnesses. In the fourteenth century, France began prosecuting unlicensed doctors.

18. **D. Swallowing a raisin with a spider in it.**

19. **C. Goose droppings.**

20. **B. Touch a dead man's tooth.**

21. **D. Keep her from aging.**

22. **A. Kiss the guest.** And then show him or her to the table. The ladies would curtsy. There were no forks used at the table. Forks were not in general use until the late fourteenth century. Spoons were provided at the meal; however, guests provided their own knives.

23. **B. Washed their hands.** A page or attendant would bring out a washbowl and a pitcher filled with water. Everyone would wash and then dry their hands on a long towel. Those not sitting at the lord's table would sit at trestle tables on benches that might also serve as their beds at night.

Middle Ages Answers (cont.)

24. **B. Thick slices of bread.** The lord, his family, and his special guests would be served from a silver platter. The others would be served from wooden platters. Two people shared a platter. The food was taken from the platters and placed on a thick slice of bread called a trencher. A trencher was shared by two people and cut in half, so each person had his own trencher, which was also used as a plate. Plates were not used in England until the end of the fourteenth century. Often, wooden bowls would be used with a thick slice of bread that lined the bottom. In other cases, round bread would be scooped out to form a bowl. After the meal, the trenchers and bowl liners were taken by the servants and were given to the poor to eat.

25. **D. Hair dryers.** Hair was often dyed during the Middle Ages, and curling irons were available to curl hair. They used hairpins made of bone, ivory, wood, silver, gold, and other kinds of metals.

26. **B. The Bean.** First, a cake was served to the men, and a cake was served to the women. In each cake, a bean or a glass bead had been inserted. Then, the man and woman who received the bean were declared to be King and Queen of the Bean. The class or social standing of the person who received the bean did not matter; they were still placed at a high table and served as if they were a lord or lady. During supper, six people disguised as oxen would run into the hall and dance around the wassail tree.

27. **D. The trees.** The people would go outside to the oldest tree, or they might bring a tree into the hall and form a circle around it. There they would toast the tree with cider. Each cup would contain three pieces of seed cake. After they toasted the tree, they would each eat one piece of cake and offer the other two pieces to the tree. Then the people would sing as they circled the tree. They would pour the rest of the cider at the tree's roots.

28. **B. Wrapping the victim in red cloth.** And then hanging other pieces of red cloth around the bed. It was thought that this not only helped the victims recover sooner, but it also would reduce pockmarks.

Name: _____ Date: _____

Medieval Fair Logic Problem

At a medieval fair, there are four booths, each of which has a different color of roof. The vendors at each of the booths has a different name, and each sells a different product or service. Look at the pictures of the booths below, read the clues and then figure out the name of each vendor, the product or service he offers for sale, the color of his roof, and the location of each booth. The word "left" means to the reader's left and the word "right" means to the reader's right.

1. William isn't a barber.

2. The man who sells the thrushes is to the right of at least two other booths.

3. Oscar and the owner of the booth with the yellow roof (which is not the second booth) are brothers.

4. The vendor selling hot sheep's feet is somewhere to the right of William but somewhere to the left of the booth with the green roof.

5. There is only one booth between Sean and the booth with the blue roof.

6. The vendor selling ale is somewhere to the right of the booth that has the red roof.

7. Geoffrey, Oscar's brother, goes to the fair early to cook his product.

8. The yellow roof is between the blue and green roofs.

Name of Vendor	Name of Product or Service	Color of Roof
1. _____	_____	_____
2. _____	_____	_____
3. _____	_____	_____
4. _____	_____	_____

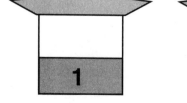 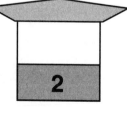 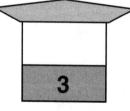 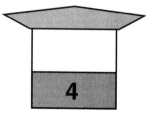

Name: _____ Date: _____

The Crusades

Jerusalem was an important city for Jews, Christians, and Muslims during the Middle Ages, just as it is today. In 1095, the Muslim Turks who held the city barred Christians. At this time, there were two Christian churches. The Western Christian Church was based in Rome, and the Eastern Christian Church was based in Constantinople. Both Christian churches were angry that they could not make pilgrimages to Jerusalem, so they joined forces to "free Jerusalem." The resulting campaign is known as the Crusades. The term Crusades generally refers to any military operations during the Middle Ages initiated by the Catholic Church or its leaders against non-Catholics. Most crusades were aimed at Muslim states in the Middle East. The Crusades began in 1096 and lasted until 1270.

Circle the letter of the answer you believe correctly completes each statement.

1. In 1032, Pope Benedict IX became pope at age:
   A. Five.
   B. Twelve.
   C. Twenty-one.
   D. Ninety-two.

2. During this period, a person could become a member of the clergy, such as a bishop or an abbot, after:
   A. Ten years of study.
   B. Living in a monastery.
   C. Passing an examination.
   D. No training at all.

3. One of the most unusual crusades was known as the:
   A. Mother's Crusade.
   B. Children's Crusade.
   C. Crusade of the Animals.
   D. Jewish Crusade.

4. Which of the following was not involved in a crusade?
   A. St. Louis
   B. St. Joan
   C. Richard the Lionhearted
   D. Walter the Penniless

5. During this period, most of the children did not survive to the age of:
   A. Five.
   B. Ten.
   C. Fifteen.
   D. Twenty.

6. During the first Crusade, about a third of those marching were:
   A. Women and children.
   B. Trained soldiers.
   C. Priests.
   D. Knights.

7. Saladin, a Muslim sultan, was so successful in battle that when he returned home:
   A. The price of slaves fell.
   B. He was made sultan for life.
   C. He was made pope.
   D. He was chosen to lead an army.

Name: _____ Date: _____

The Crusades (cont.)

8. Finding which of the following is **not** considered motivation for Columbus and others to discover and explore the New World?
   A. A trade route to the East   B. Gold
   C. A route for the conquest of Jerusalem   D. Tobacco

9. When the Muslims planned their battles with the Franks, they wanted the battle to:
   A. Last a long time.   B. Be fought at sunrise.
   C. Be on horseback.   D. Be in the winter.

10. In 1098, the crusaders in Antioch refused to obey their commanders and fight. When the commanders heard of this, they:
   A. Killed them.   B. Had them excommunicated.
   C. Made them slaves.   D. Set their houses on fire.

11. During the first Crusade, more than half of the peasants who marched were armed with:
   A. Nothing.   B. Bows and arrows.
   C. Swords.   D. Clubs.

12. Pope Urban II made a powerful and persuasive speech encouraging his listeners to join the first Crusade by telling them that by doing so:
   A. They would not have to pay tax.   B. They could visit the Holy Land.
   C. All of their sins would be forgiven.   D. They would be made saints.

13. One of the most interesting leaders of the Crusades was a man known as:
   A. Peter the Great.   B. Peter the Hermit.
   C. Sneaky Pete.   D. Peter the Knight.

14. Another interesting leader of the Crusades was a man known as:
   A. Walter the Thunderer.   B. Walter the Woodsman.
   C. Walter the Penniless.   D. Walter Two Fingers.

15. Before the eleventh century, it was common for priests to be:
   A. Married.   B. Women.
   C. Jewish.   D. Soldiers.

16. During the Crusades, there was a group of Germanic people living in the lower and middle Rhine Valley called Franks. A Frank's home was called a:
   A. Palace.   B. Hovel.
   C. Hut.   D. Castle.

80

The Crusades Answers

1. **B. Twelve.**
2. **D. No training at all.** Becoming a member of the clergy, such as a bishop or abbot, was a way to become wealthy and powerful. High-ranking church officials were often lords who had a great deal of land. Dukes and counts, who chose the bishops and abbots within their own counties, frequently named family members or friends to positions in the clergy, even though they might not have had any religious training.
3. **B. Children's Crusade.** In June 1212, a shepherd boy named Stephen said that he had a vision of Jesus who commanded him to raise an army to go to the Holy Land. Many of Stephen's fellow shepherds accompanied Stephen to Paris to see the king. They carried banners, crosses, and candles chanting, "Lord God, exalt Christianity! Lord God, restore to us the True Cross." When they arrived in Paris, King Philip II apparently convinced them to give up and go home. Also, in the spring of 1212, a boy named Nicholas began another children's crusade. Unfortunately, many of the children who went on this Crusade died of illnesses, starvation, and injuries. As they were traveling to the Holy Land, many of the remaining children were captured and sold into slavery.
4. **B. St. Joan.**
5. **A. Five.** During this time, it was a man's world. Women mostly spent their life either preparing to be married or after they were married, bearing children. People understood that many of their children would not survive. This fact was accepted as a part of life. Marriages in the upper classes were arranged. It was not uncommon for children of the upper classes to be married when they were five or six years old, so they could be married into a desirable family. Sometimes, a child might be married to a much older adult in order to join two families and form a dynasty. For example, Baldwin III of Jerusalem married a Byzantine princess named Theodora. He was 27 years old, and she was 13 years old.
6. **A. Women and children.**
7. **A. The price of slaves fell.** He captured so many that when he sold them into slavery, the price of slaves fell very low; the market had become overloaded.
8. **D. Tobacco.**
9. **A. Last a long time.** One of the advantages that the Franks had over the Muslims was their superior armor. However, the Muslims soon learned that the armor, while protecting the Franks, was heavy and hot. Fighting over a long period of time wore the Franks out, so the Muslims planned their battles so they would take a long time.
10. **D. Set their houses on fire.** With no place to hide, the men had to come out and fight.
11. **A. Nothing.** They had no weapons nor military training. Only a small number had been trained as soldiers or archers. The most common weapon carried by crusaders was a double-sided ax.
12. **C. All of their sins would be forgiven.** And they would be assured of a reward in the kingdom of heaven.

The Crusades Answers (cont.)

13. **B. Peter the Hermit.** Peter the Hermit had taken vows of poverty. Dressing himself in peasant's clothing and riding a donkey throughout France and Germany, he encouraged people to join the crusade. He ultimately assembled over 40,000 men, women, and children willing to follow him.

14. **C. Walter the Penniless.** During the same crusade as Peter the Hermit, there was another leader, a French monk, whose name was Walter the Penniless. Along with Peter the Hermit, the two of them were eventually able to assemble over 70,000, mostly poor and uneducated people, to march to Constantinople on a crusade.

15. **A. Married.** Leo IX commanded that priests not marry, and he publicly excommunicated noblemen and church officials who had become church officials by bribery.

16. **A. Palace.** Franks' homes were built on tops of hills so they could be defended easily. Also, the wind made the house cooler in the summer. Many who lived in towns lived in single-story houses or houses with two floors, which were called palaces. There were square rooms on two floors surrounded by a central patio which was apart from the main entrance. All the doors and windows opened to the patio.

Name: _____ Date: _____

Knights of the Crusades Logic Problem

On their way to the Crusades, four knights sat at a round table in the positions 1, 2, 3, and 4 as shown below. Read the clues and determine the name of each knight, what each ate and drank, and where each sat.

Knights: Cedric, Geoffrey, Richard, and William
Drinks: Ale, Beer, Tea, and Mead
Food: Biscuits, Bread, Cake, and Crackers

Clues:

1. The knight who drank the mead also ate the cake. He was not Cedric.

2. The knight in seat #3 ate crackers.

3. Richard sat opposite the knight who drank beer.

4. Tea was drunk by the knight in seat #4. This knight was not William.

5. The person who drank the beer was not one place clockwise from Geoffrey.

6. Geoffrey was sitting between the knight who drank the ale and the knight who ate the bread.

7. The knight who drank the ale did not eat biscuits.

1

Name: _____

Drink: _____

Food: _____

1

4   **2**

3

2

Name: _____

Drink: _____

Food: _____

4

Name: _____

Drink: _____

Food: _____

3

Name: _____

Drink: _____

Food: _____

Name: _____   Date: _____

Family Coat of Arms Logic Problem

Shown below is a picture of a coat of arms used by a knight in the Crusades. The coat of arms had four sections. On each section was a symbol of a different color. The background colors for each of the four sections were different as well. You are to figure out the colors of each of the symbols and the colors of each of the backgrounds.

The following colors can be found somewhere in the shield: blue, gold, green, gray, pink, red, silver, and white. No color is used more than once.

Clues:

1. The oak leaf is green and it is in section two.

2. One of the four sections has a red symbol on a gold background. It is not in section four.

3. There is no white or silver in section one. In fact, these two colors are not in the same section at all. One is the color of a symbol and the other is the color of a background.

4. Silver is the color of one of the symbols.

5. The blue background is in the lower half of the coat of arms. The symbol shown on this background is not gray.

6. The section with the gray coloring is just a little left of the one with pink. One of these is a background color; the other is the color of a symbol.

Name: _____ Date: _____

The Renaissance

The Renaissance is a period in history that marked a "re-birth" of classical knowledge, art, and learning that developed in Europe, especially in Italy. The Renaissance began during the fourteenth century and lasted until the sixteenth century.

Circle the letter of the answer(s) you believe correctly completes each statement.

1. From 1500 to 1650, women often went to church dressed in:
   A. Armor.
   B. Rags.
   C. Men's clothes.
   D. Their nightgowns.

2. In order to avoid the plague, a common treatment was to drink four ounces of:
   A. Rat's blood.
   B. Gin.
   C. Mummy.
   D. Swamp water.

3. During the Renaissance, in order to protect themselves from the sun, some people wore:
   A. Sunglasses.
   B. Masks.
   C. Sunscreen.
   D. Chicken fat.

4. During the Renaissance, it was thought that epilepsy could be cured by drinking spring water at night from:
   A. A cup that had been blessed.
   B. The skull of a murder victim.
   C. A maiden's shoe.
   D. A knight's helmet.

5. When onboard, sailors could be whipped or lashed for:
   A. Throwing garbage overboard.
   B. Spitting overboard.
   C. Singing after midnight.
   D. Stealing lemons.

6. Who wore girdles in the 1500s?
   A. Men
   B. Women
   C. Men and women
   D. Priests

7. Sailors often bragged about the fact that they:
   A. Were not able to swim.
   B. Had many tattoos.
   C. Had sailed around the world.
   D. Could hold their breath for four minutes.

8. Those sent to prisons usually were:
   A. Sent there for life.
   B. Allowed to leave whenever they wanted.
   C. Kept in chains.
   D. Dead within a year.

Name: _____ Date: _____

The Renaissance (cont.)

9. On the battlements on London Bridge were a number of poles. On these poles were:
   A. Flags.
   B. Sentries from Warsaw.
   C. Severed heads of traitors.
   D. Acrobats.

10. A postal system was established in London in 1482. If a "postboy" was carrying a letter that was urgent, it was marked with a:
    A. Red stamp.
    B. King's seal.
    C. Drawing of a man on the gallows.
    D. Drawing of a speeding horse.

11. Grace O'Malley of Ireland was one of the best known:
    A. Archers.
    B. Pirates.
    C. Queens.
    D. Witches.

12. When King Henry VIII took his army to France, what did he **not** take along with him?
    A. A wooden house
    B. His court
    C. A fireplace
    D. A list of the best French restaurants

13. Church towers were sometimes used as:
    A. Astronomical observatories.
    B. Nunneries.
    C. A home for friars.
    D. Beehives.

14. It was common for someone to be sentenced to prison because of:
    A. A debt.
    B. Spitting in the street.
    C. Eating fish on Sunday.
    D. Whistling in church.

15. These products were called "white meats."
    A. Chicken
    B. Milk
    C. Pork
    D. Sheep

16. Aboard ship, the boatswain scheduled this event every Monday morning.
    A. Work assignments
    B. Weekly devotionals
    C. Lashing
    D. Choir practice

17. Who had the healthiest diet during the Renaissance?
    A. Royalty
    B. Wealthy people
    C. Clergymen
    D. The poor

18. Which of the following services did the barbers provide during the Renaissance?
    A. Cut hair
    B. Collected blood
    C. Cleaned teeth
    D. Pierced ears

Name: _____ Date: _____

The Renaissance (cont.)

19. During Elizabethan times, clothes were washed:
    A. Never.
    B. Once a year.
    C. Once a month.
    D. Weekly.

20. During the Renaissance, people sometimes wore a pomander. A pomander was:
    A. A hairstyle.
    B. A hat.
    C. Used to make them smell good.
    D. A wig.

21. During the Renaissance when a young man was courting a girl, he generally gave her a _____ on their first date.
    A. Dove
    B. Ring
    C. Flower
    D. A list of his assets and titles

22. When someone was invited for dinner, they usually brought their own _____.
    A. Plates
    B. Food
    C. Knives
    D. Wine

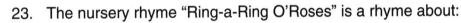

23. The nursery rhyme "Ring-a-Ring O'Roses" is a rhyme about:
    A. The Crusades.
    B. Queen Rosemary.
    C. The plague.
    D. Joan of Arc.

24. Most houses, even palaces, had _____ on the floor.
    A. Carpets
    B. Rushes and reeds
    C. Mosaic tile
    D. Felt-covered planks

25. What drink was served to everyone at most breakfasts?
    A. Tea
    B. Water
    C. Mare's milk
    D. Beer

26. The word "hospital" during this time referred to a shelter for:
    A. Sick people.
    B. Criminals.
    C. Homeless people.
    D. People who were insane.

27. During the Renaissance, most Italian women had:
    A. Black hair.
    B. Brown hair.
    C. Blonde hair.
    D. No hair.

The Renaissance Answers

1. **D. Their nightgowns.** While nightgowns were usually used at home as dressing gowns, they were frequently worn outside the house and at special events. Nightgowns had long sleeves and covered the ankles. They were made of silk, satin, velvet, and may have even been trimmed with fur.

2. **C. Mummy.** In order to avoid the plague, a common treatment was to drink four ounces of mummy that had been mixed with wine and other herbs. Mummy, of course, was the dried flesh of a dead person. The patient was required to drink this mixture as he was wearing a bag of arsenic and burning old shoes. The smoke from the burning shoes was thought to purify the air.

3. **B. Masks.** Masks were often worn to protect the wearer from the sun. Sometimes they were worn to hide the person's identity.

4. **B. The skull of a murder victim.**

5. **D. Stealing lemons.** Scurvy is a disease caused by a lack of vitamin C. Among other things, it causes loosening of the teeth and joint and bone pain. Scurvy was a serious problem among sailors because fruits and vegetables, which prevented this disease, would spoil on a lengthy sea voyage. Ships generally carried lemons to cure those who were most severely impacted by this disease. Stealing these lemons was like stealing valuable medicine.

6. **C. Men and women.** In the 1500s, both men and women wore girdles.

7. **A. Were not able to swim.** Those who could swim were accused of not having faith in the captain or the ship's ability to return to port.

8. **B. Allowed to leave whenever they wanted.** Prisons were different than they are today. It was possible to get a furlough from prison and then return at a later time. In fact, a prisoner could leave prison for up to a year if they were able to pay enough bail. They could also leave for a shorter length of time as long as they would pay the wages of a prison official to accompany them. Prisoners sometimes hired other prisoners as servants.

9. **C. Severed heads of traitors.** In order to preserve the heads, they were parboiled, dipped in tar, and left on the poles until they decayed. The heads were displayed this way to discourage others from committing treason.

10. **C. Drawing of a man on the gallows.** This was a clue for the postboy to deliver the letter as quickly as if it were a pardon.

11. **B. Pirates.** She was captured twice and sentenced to hang but was pardoned by the queen of England.

The Renaissance Answers (cont.)

12. **D. A list of the best French restaurants.** He took along a wooden, portable house that was stored in several different carts. It could be assembled quickly at any location. It had two rooms, a fireplace, and a chimney. In other carts were a number of tents that when assembled with the house provided the king and his entourage several rooms with 4,000 square feet of living space. He also brought along his own bed and other furniture.

13. **D. Beehives.** Most farmers and other people kept bees as a source for honey, which was used as a sweetener. Many different structures were used for beehives, including church towers.

14. **A. A debt.** It was common for someone to be sentenced to prison because of a debt, which really makes little sense. If a person were imprisoned, how could they ever pay the debt? Some people chose to go to prison in order to keep their possessions for their heirs. Once a person died, all of his debts were canceled. In fact, there are some cases of people who borrowed money, invested it, intentionally went bankrupt, and were sent to prison. While in prison, they were able to live comfortably by hiring other prisoners as servants, receiving family members for visits, enjoying good food, and passing along a substantial inheritance from their investments when they died.

15. **B. Milk.** Dairy products were called "white meats." All of the products in this category, which included milk, cream, curds, whey, cheese, and eggs were only eaten by the poor. The rich people considered these as inferior foods.

16. **C. Lashing.**

17. **D. The poor.** In the middle of the sixteenth century, vegetables were generally eaten only by the poor. The only vegetables wealthy people occasionally ate were onions, leeks, and garlic. They mainly ate meat and pastry. Poor people ate little meat but a wide variety of vegetables, cheeses, and breads. They had a vegetable they called the "potato." It was what we call the sweet potato today. The white potato that we know today was referred to as the "potato of America." This type of potato was not generally raised as a food until a few centuries after the Renaissance. Butter was common, but the rich usually used it only for cooking, while the poor put butter on their food. In England, almost everyone suffered from some sort of malnutrition or vitamin deficiency. Most people suffered from a vitamin C deficiency.

18. **All answers are correct.** Barbers were very different in the Renaissance than they are today. They were known as barbers/surgeons because they performed some medical duties. Barbers not only cut and trimmed hair, mustaches and beards, they also collected blood, pierced ears, cleaned teeth, and had other medical duties.

19. **B. Once a year.** Clothes were not washed very often during the Elizabethan times, usually only once or twice a year. They were sometimes brushed or beaten with wooden sticks between washings to remove the lice.

20. **C. Used to make them smell good.** People living in this period did not bathe often and did not wash their clothes. Consequently, body odor was a problem. A pomander was a hollow perforated ball that people wore to cover up the smell of their bodies and clothes. Inside the pomander was a ball of wax mixed with some type of perfume. The

The Renaissance Answers (cont.)

pomander was often made of precious metal and decorated with jewels. Women attached them to their girdles, while men wore them on a chain around their necks.

21. **B. Ring.** Courting varied from time to time and from place to place. However, it was common for a boy who wanted to court a girl to first write a letter to the girl's father asking permission to court the daughter. If he was granted the father's permission, the boy gave her a ring on the first visit; then each time he would visit her, he would bring her a gift until they were married.

22. **C. Knives.** When someone was invited for dinner, they usually brought their own knives.

23. **C. The plague.** While the song began in London during the seventeenth century, it referred to the Black Death that killed over 25 million during the fourteenth century. Here is what each line meant: *Ring-a-ring O'roses:* those infected with the plague developed red rashes the color of roses. *Pocket full of posies:* people thought the plague and other illnesses were caused by the poisoned breath of demons. A pocket full of flowers or sweet- smelling herbs would protect a person from the poisoned breath and the plague. *Atishoo! Atishoo!* (This is the original phrase, but today children say, *"Ashes! Ashes!"*) When a person caught the plague, they sneezed, and it sounded like, "Atishoo." *We all fall down:* millions fell down and died of the plague.

    Some ways to stop the plague: people went around whipping themselves as a penance to God. Some people accused Jews of poisoning wells and attacked them. One of the reasons the plague was so widespread was because people believed that those who owned cats were witches; in many places, cats were rounded up and killed. However, rats who carried the disease-causing parasites were free to multiply.

24. **B. Rushes and reeds.** Most people used carpets as decorations; they put them on tables and on cupboards. Because they were very expensive, few people put them on the floors. Most houses, even palaces, threw rushes and reeds mixed with various scented flowers and petals on the floor.

25. **D. Beer.** During the Renaissance, people generally ate three meals a day. The staples of their diet were beef, bread, and beer. Depending on a person's wealth, breakfast might consist of beef, lamb, pottage, fish, butter, and beer; even children drank beer for breakfast. From the middle of the 16th century, beer was a popular drink in Europe. Beer was so popular that when William Cecil, Lord Cranborne, was on a tour of Europe, he brought along his own brewer, because he thought that he could not find good beer in other countries. People thought that milk caused headaches and sore eyes. The only ones who drank milk were children and old people. Most of the milk produced was used to make cheese. During this period, tea was not generally available in England. People drank water very little, because most of the water sources were polluted.

26. **All answers are correct.** The word "hospital" during this time referred to a shelter. Only a few hospitals actually took care of sick people.

27. **C. Blonde hair.** During the Renaissance, blonde hair became so popular that only the working classes had brown or black hair.

Name: _____ Date: _____

The Inquisition

Established by the pope in the Middle Ages, the Inquisition attempted to find, try, and sentence those people guilty of heresy. **Heresy** is any religious belief or practice opposed to a particular church. In this case, it meant anyone that did not believe or practice the Catholic religion. The original penalty for heresy was excommunication; however, when Christianity became the state religion in the fourth century, heretics came to be considered enemies of the state. Heresy then became a crime against the state.

The inquisitors, who had assistants and the police to help them, would set up at a central location and issue an order that all guilty of heresy must come and confess. Those who came forward and confessed had milder penalties than those who didn't. Those who were accused of heresy and didn't come forward went to trial. If the inquisitors thought a suspect was lying, they could put him in prison and have him tortured.

Of course, many accused of heresy were not guilty of anything. A neighbor or enemy would secretly report that a person was a heretic. The accused then went on trial and had to prove that he was innocent, which was almost impossible. For many, a simple accusation by an enemy would mean years in prison and torture unless they confessed.

The sentences for those who confessed or were found guilty were announced publicly. The sentence might be some type of service to a hospital or monastery, or it might be a flogging or the wearing of a cross. If the heresy was considered serious enough, a person's property was taken away, or he could be sent to prison. The church could not execute anyone, but in severe cases, it would hand the prisoner to a civil court to be executed.

When people hear the word *Inquisition,* most think of the Spanish Inquisition, but the Inquisition took place in many countries. It even occurred in the New World in the Spanish colonies.

Circle the letter of the answer(s) you believe correctly completes each statement.

1. A person could be charged with heresy for all but one of the following. Which one?
   A. Not eating pork   B. Not drinking alcohol
   C. Not bathing   D. Smiling at the name of the Virgin Mary

2. Prisoners found guilty of heresy were forced to march in a procession and wear a(n):
   A. Dunce's cap.   B. Upside-down cross.
   C. Letter "H" on his forehead.   D. Mask of a devil.

3. Galileo was accused of heresy because he believed:
   A. Jesus was not the son of God.   B. The sun was the center of the universe.
   C. In the theory of evolution.   D. Protestantism.

4. Just before a prisoner was to be executed, he was given the opportunity to confess. If he did confess, the public officials would have mercy on him and:
   A. Set him free.   B. Give him a life sentence.
   C. Baptize him.   D. Strangle him.

Name: _____ Date: _____

The Inquisition (cont.)

5. Which of the following was not a type of torture typically used during the Inquisition?
   - A. Stretching the prisoner
   - B. Burning the prisoner
   - C. Chinese water torture
   - D. Filling the prisoner with water

6. In 1252, Pope Innocent IV issued a decree:
   - A. Forbidding torture.
   - B. Approving torture.
   - C. Forbidding imprisonment.
   - D. Forbidding priests from being inquisitors.

7. Most accused of heresy defended themselves because:
   - A. There were no lawyers.
   - B. Lawyers wouldn't defend them.
   - C. They had no money.
   - D. Lawyers were not allowed to defend them.

8. It was possible for someone to be brought to trial and to have his property confiscated even though he:
   - A. Was found innocent.
   - B. Had no money or property.
   - C. Was dead.
   - D. Was charged with a minor crime.

9. The person who tortured the prisoners was usually a:
   - A. Priest.
   - B. Mayor.
   - C. Soldier.
   - D. Jailer.

10. In the Spanish colonies of the New World, the term "Lutheran" meant:
    - A. Protestant.
    - B. Any new religious belief.
    - C. Those who followed Martin Luther.
    - D. Jews.

11. In the Spanish colonies of the Americas, the term "foreigner" meant:
    - A. Protestant.
    - B. Any new religious belief.
    - C. Those who followed Martin Luther.
    - D. Jews.

12. Spain issued several decrees barring _____ from going to the Spanish colonies in the New World.
    - A. Married men
    - B. Priests
    - C. Jews and Moors
    - D. Women

13. In the New World, the main job of the lawyer of a man being tried for heresy was to:
    - A. Have the jury find his client innocent.
    - B. Save his client from a death sentence.
    - C. Save his client from prison.
    - D. Get his client to plead guilty.

14. Those who confessed to heresy in the Americas were allowed to return to the church, but they could not become:
    - A. Druggists.
    - B. Grocers.
    - C. Bleeders.
    - D. Lawyers.

The Inquisition Answers

1. **C. Not bathing.** While not bathing may be unhealthy and not pleasant to those around, it was not considered heresy unless it was a ritual bath of purification. To the inquisitor, a person who refused to eat pork might be a Jew practicing his religion secretly. Someone who refused to drink alcohol might be a Muslim. A person might be accused of heresy even if he smiled slightly when the name of the Virgin Mary was uttered.

2. **A. Dunce's cap.** The procession included trumpeters, drummers, priests, local officials, judges, the bishop and men carrying lighted candles and crosses. The condemned wore a tunic with a red cross on it. Many of the condemned had their heads shaved, and some had to wear a dunce's cap, which was a symbol of a Jew.

3. **B. The sun was the center of the universe.** The Church taught that the earth was the center of the universe. Galileo was brought before the Roman Inquisition in 1632 and questioned at length. When he was questioned, he retracted (took back) his statement and said that he really believed the earth was the center of the universe and promised never to say otherwise again.

4. **D. Strangle him.** When the procession of the condemned reached the designated spot, there was a sermon and a reading of the names of those to be punished. There would be an explanation of the crimes committed and a reading of the sentence. Some received relatively mild punishments, while others were executed. If the person had recanted his sins, he might only be punished by having to wear a tunic with a red cross on it. This would be a constant reminder to everyone that they should not commit the same crime. Other prisoners might be flogged or put in prison. Those convicted of very serious crimes might be released, only to be taken to a civil court and sentenced to death, since the church did not sentence people to death. If a person was sentenced to death and at the last minute confessed his crimes and asked for forgiveness, the public officials would have mercy on him and strangle him before he was burned alive.

5. **C. Chinese water torture.** Torture was not considered a punishment; it was used to get confessions of those who were accused. Many different kinds of torture were used. A prisoner might be hung upside-down. Sometimes a victim was placed on a rack and stretched. He might even be burned while being stretched. Keeping a prisoner awake for a great length of time was used to gain confessions. Sometimes a long rope was used to tie a victim's hands behind his back, and the other end was thrown over a beam in the ceiling. The prisoner was drawn up and weights were placed on his feet. Another type of torture was called the leg-screw. The prisoner's leg was put in a device consisting of two pieces of metal which pressed together when a screw was turned. The inquisitor turned the screw until the leg was crushed. Another method of torture was dousing a prisoner's feet with a liquid that would burn and then lighting it. The victim could be placed on his back and filled with water.

6. **B. Approving torture.** While torture was permitted, priests were reminded they should not spill blood and they could only torture a suspect once. However, inquisitors were able to get around this restriction of torturing only once by torturing a victim and throwing him back into the cell. Then when they tortured him later, they claimed it was just a continuation of the first torturing, not a new one. They would repeat this process until

The Inquisition Answers (cont.)

the inquisitor was able to get a confession. When a person made a confession under torture, he was required to leave the torture chamber and repeat the confession to a clerk, since confessions made during torture were not valid. If the punishment for the crime was death, the priest would have to turn the prisoner over to the civil authorities to carry out the judgement.

7. **B. Lawyers wouldn't defend them.** While lawyers were available during the Inquisition and prisoners had a right to use one, few did. It was the general belief that if a lawyer defended a heretic, he must also be a heretic. It followed that if he were a heretic, then the arguments he used to defend the accused must be lies. Not only would the lawyer's client be found guilty, the lawyer would be found guilty as well.

8. **C. Was dead.** Confiscation of property applied only to those cases where the accused was able to escape the inquisition or died. There were many cases where a person had been dead for many years and then was judged to be a heretic. The dead man needed to go through the same parade as those who were alive went through. His corpse was dug up and paraded through city streets and his name and offenses were read in public. The dead heretic's property was confiscated from his heirs. It did not matter if the heirs were good practicing Catholics and committed no crime or no heresy. If it was judged that the person who had willed them their property and money was a heretic before he died, their inheritance was taken.

9. **A. A priest.** When the inquisition began, it was originally felt that priests should not be involved in torture. Therefore, people who were not priests were given the job of torturing prisoners. After a while, however, it was decided that it was inconvenient to have those other than priests to conduct the questioning and the torture.

10. **B. Any new religious belief.** There were inquisitors in the Americas, and they were concerned that the native people might become Protestants. The term "Lutheran" came to mean all new religious beliefs.

11. **A. Protestant.**

12. **C. Jews and Moors.**

13. **D. Get his client to plead guilty.** In the New World, unlike Europe, those accused of heresy often used a lawyer. The inquisitor designated three lawyers from which the accused might choose. Instead of defending his client, the lawyer's main purpose was to convince the defendant to plead guilty. Unlike modern trials in the United States, those accusing the defendant did not have the responsibility of proving him guilty. In other words, the defendant was not considered innocent until proved guilty as he is in the United States. The defendant was guilty unless he was able to prove himself innocent. If he was not able to prove himself innocent, he was found guilty.

14. **All answers are correct.** The laws were slightly different in the colonies of the New World as compared to those in Europe. In the Americas, those who confessed had their funds confiscated. They were required to wear a tunic with a red cross on it. They might be given lashes or required to serve as oarsmen on galleys. They would also have to fast on certain days, say prayers, and attend mass. They could not become physicians, surgeons, merchants, lawyers, druggists, or grocers.

Name: _____ Date: _____

The Age of Reason and the French Revolution

From the latter part of the seventeenth century to the beginning of the nineteenth century, there is a period that is often referred to as the Age of Reason. Throughout Europe and the American colonies, philosophers, scholars and writers were questioning government, religion, and the composition of the universe. The more people thought about these matters, the more they desired to change them. There was a gradual feeling that ordinary individuals had rights. Some of these rights included a voice in their government, the right to an education, the right not to be tortured or made a slave, and the right to freely voice an opinion. France was no exception to this feeling that was sweeping many countries in the world. Eventually, the people of France became angry with the extravagant lifestyle of the king, high taxes, and their own poverty. What followed is known as the French Revolution.

Circle the letter of the answer you believe correctly completes each statement.

1. King Louis XV had a secret:
    A. Wife.
    C. Bedroom.
        B. That he was bald.
        D. Handshake.

2. When Louis XV was 15 years old, he broke his engagement to a Spanish princess who was:
    A. His cousin.
    C. His stepsister.
        B. Seven years old.
        D. A bullfighter.

3. Louis XIV was a:
    A. Ballet dancer.
    C. Playwright.
        B. Trombonist.
        D. Olympic champion.

4. Before the Age of Reason, it was common for women to send their children to the country for two years so they could:
    A. Enjoy the clean country air.
    C. Learn the skills needed for life.
        B. Be protected from crime.
        D. Be breast-fed.

5. During the Age of Reason, if a person committed suicide in France, the corpse was:
    A. Burned.
    C. Used by medical students.
        B. Hanged.
        D. Buried upside-down.

6. When a woman took a bath in a bathtub, she might:
    A. Wear a dress.
    C. Bathe with a friend.
        B. Stay in all day.
        D. Not get wet.

7. Which of the following was not a responsibility of the chief of police in France during the Age of Reason?
    A. Selling lottery tickets
    C. Finding stray pets
        B. Lighting the streets
        D. Conscripting men for the militia

The Age of Reason and the French Revolution (cont.)

8. Each year during this period, about 4,000 of these were abandoned in Paris:
   A. Newborn infants.
   B. Elderly parents.
   C. Wives.
   D. Snakes.

9. Male tennis players wore:
   A. Dresses.
   B. Nothing.
   C. Hairnets.
   D. Girdles.

10. King Louis XV liked to:
    A. Cut out paper dolls.
    B. Walk along the rooftops of the palace.
    C. Present puppet shows.
    D. Teach his old dog new tricks.

11. When a person was at court, it was easy to tell how important he was by:
    A. His hairstyle.
    B. His chair.
    C. How he spoke.
    D. His shoes.

12. In the palace when someone wanted to enter a room, they would:
    A. Knock at the door.
    B. Scratch at the door.
    C. Bang their head on the door.
    D. Just enter.

13. King Louis XV once went to a costume ball as:
    A. A tree.
    B. Louis the XIV.
    C. His wife.
    D. Himself.

14. When a woman put on her makeup, she would also put on:
    A. False tattoos.
    B. Fake eyebrows.
    C. False beauty marks.
    D. False fingernails.

15. During the eighteenth century when upperclass women rode in a carriage, they:
    A. Rode alone.
    B. Wrapped a towel around their head.
    C. Wore a mask.
    D. Put their heads out the window.

16. When King Louis XV died, he was buried in:
    A. A robe of ermine and pearls.
    B. A pauper's cemetery.
    C. An ivory casket.
    D. Two lead caskets.

17. Dr. Joseph Guillotine encouraged the French government to use a machine that cut off people's heads because:
    A. It was a fast way to execute.
    B. It was painless.
    C. It was easier than other methods.
    D. He disliked aristocrats.

The Age of Reason and the French Revolution Answers

1. **C. Bedroom.** The State Bedchamber was large, drafty, and uncomfortable. Louis would not sleep there. When the king was to retire for the night, he was accompanied to his bedchamber by a number of people. The Gentleman of the Bedchamber would hand him his nightclothes; then, someone would carry a candle to light the King's way to bed. After everyone left, Louis would get up and go to his other, more comfortable bedchamber. It was a suite of fifty rooms and seven bathrooms called Petits Appartements and was known and visited by only a few guests.

2. **B. Seven years old.** He broke the engagement and married Marie Leszczynska.

3. **A. Ballet dancer.** Even when he was older, paintings of him show him opening his robe to show off his attractive legs.

4. **D. Be breast-fed.** During the Age of Reason, middle-class families began to breast-feed their own children. Before that, it was common for mothers to send their babies to the country for two years, so they could send their children to be nursed.

5. **B. Hanged.** The corpse would be taken naked through the streets and then publicly hanged.

6. **A. Wear a dress.** She might do this to protect her from touching the metal of the tub.

7. **C. Finding stray pets.**

8. **A. Newborn infants.** They were left on the streets of Paris or on a church's steps.

9. **C. Hairnets.** Since men had their hair curled and perfumed, they did not want to mess it up when they played a game of tennis.

10. **B. Walk along the rooftops of the palace.** He spent much of his time carving ivory but also enjoyed walking along the rooftops of the palace. He would jump in through a window and surprise his ministers or other guests. On one occasion, he even entered a room through a chimney.

11. **B. His chair.** When the king held court, the most important people were allowed to sit in a chair. Those who weren't quite as important would sit on a stool. Those of even lesser importance would not be permitted to sit down at all.

12. **B. Scratch at the door.** It was the custom.

13. **A. A tree.** So he could walk around costume balls unnoticed, Louis would have several people in his same costume. He once dressed as a tree and had seven other men dress as identical trees.

14. **C. False beauty marks.** The beauty marks came in several different shapes. They were shaped like moons, stars, teardrops, hearts, or just plain dots.

15. **D. Put their heads out the window.** Their hairstyles were so high that they had to kneel or put their heads out the window so they could fit in the carriage. In some cases, staircases had to be redesigned for women with the new, tall hairstyle.

16. **D. Two lead caskets.** Since King Louis XV died of smallpox, his body was put into two lead caskets and placed in a crypt. The official funeral took place with an empty coffin.

17. **B. It was painless.** Before the guillotine was used in France, only the wealthy and aristocracy condemned to death had the privilege of being decapitated or beheaded. Dr. Guillotine felt that everyone put to death should be treated humanely and killed painlessly. While Guillotine's intentions were good, the consequences of having a machine that executed people so quickly made it easy to kill more people.

97

Name: _____ Date: _____

Scrambled Headlines From the Middle Ages and Beyond

     Shown below are several headlines that could have appeared in the Middle Ages if there had been newspapers. The only problem is that they are mixed up. Each headline has been broken into three parts. Each part is shown in one of three columns. Columns two and three have been scrambled. Begin with the name in the first column, and then find one phrase from the second column and one phrase from the third column to complete each headline. Write the completed headlines on the form on the following page. You may mark off the phrases as you use them. The first headline is given as an example.

1. ~~French mobs~~	sailing on the *Mayflower*	land in Plymouth
2. William Shakespeare	discovers a new world	and massacre Turks
3. Joan of Arc,	develops movable type	at the Globe Theater
4. Johann Gutenberg	a devastating epidemic,	~~killing the Swiss Guards~~
5. Mohammed,	names the Pacific Ocean	builds Peking
6. Christopher Columbus	a Polish astronomer,	is burned at the stake
7. Magellan	enter Jerusalem	to print manuscripts more cheaply
8. Cornwallis	grandson of Genghis Khan,	for selling pardons for sin
9. Louis XVI and Marie Antoinette	~~attack Bastille,~~	at Waterloo
10. Martin Luther	founder of Islam,	during French Revolution
11. Duke of Wellington	convicted of witchcraft,	by sailing west
12. Black Death,	presents Hamlet	is born in Mecca on April 20, 571
13. Crusaders	attacks Catholic Church	on a trip around the globe
14. Copernicus,	defeats Napoleon	kills 25 million
15. Pilgrims	are beheaded for treason	to George Washington
16. Kublai Khan,	surrenders at Yorktown	says sun is center of the universe

Name: _____ Date: _____

Scrambled Headlines From the Middle Ages and Beyond (cont.)

Write the completed headlines from page 98 on the lines below. The first one has been done for you.

1. *French mobs attack Bastille, killing the Swiss Guards* _____

2. _____

3. _____

4. _____

5. _____

6. _____

7. _____

8. _____

9. _____

10. _____

11. _____

12. _____

13. _____

14. _____

15. _____

16. _____

Name: _____ Date: _____

The *Titanic*

In 1898, fourteen years before the *Titanic* sank, a man named Morgan Robertson wrote a novel called *Futility.* What is amazing about this novel is that much of the story he created as fiction was eerily similar to what eventually happened to the *Titanic.* In his novel, the ship was an elaborate passenger liner, the largest to have ever been built. People in the novel said that the ship was unsinkable. The ship was sailing in the month of April across the North Atlantic with many rich and well-known passengers aboard. The ship struck an iceberg and sank. Hundreds of passengers died because there were not enough lifeboats. Perhaps the most bizarre coincidence was that the name of the ship in Robertson's novel was the *Titan.*

The *Titanic* Disaster is not the worst maritime disaster in history. Other disasters have claimed more lives, but the story of the *Titanic* still captures the imagination of people today. It was a luxury liner, which people thought could not be sunk. It was making its first voyage with some of the world's richest and most influential people aboard. There had been opportunities to avoid disaster but instead, shortly before midnight on April 14, 1912, the ship struck an iceberg and sank. Approximately 1,513 people, out of more than 2,220 aboard, perished.

As a result of the *Titanic's* disaster, modern cruise ships are required to not only have enough lifeboats for everyone aboard, but they are required to have enough lifeboats to carry 25% more than the total passengers and crew.

In 1914, two years after the *Titanic* sank, the International Ice Patrol was created. It is directed by the United States Coast Guard; its purpose is to investigate and track iceberg movements in the Northwest Atlantic where ships sail. Every April 15th, the International Ice Patrol drops a wreath on the spot where the *Titanic* sank. The wreath is provided by the Titanic Historical Society.

No lives have been lost in the North Atlantic due to ice since the *Titanic* sank.

Circle the letter of the answer you believe correctly completes each statement.

1. One famous *Titanic* passenger was Margaret Tobin Brown from Denver, who was married to a man that had made his fortune in mining. Her friends called her:
   A. Margaret.
   C. Unsinkable Molly.
   B. Molly.
   D. Maggie.

2. The dining rooms on the *Titanic* were called:
   A. Supper clubs.
   C. Table boards.
   B. Bistros.
   D. Dining saloons.

3. When the *Titanic* left the dock in Southhampton:
   A. It was on fire.
   C. One propeller was not working.
   B. The paint on the hull was still wet.
   D. It hit another ship.

4. The funnels on the *Titanic* were:
   A. Twenty stories high.
   C. Used to store cargo.
   B. All fake.
   D. Big enough to drive two trains through.

Name: _____ Date: _____

The *Titanic* (cont.)

5. How much electric cable was there on the *Titanic*?
   A. One mile
   B. Ten miles
   C. 100 miles
   D. 200 miles

6. In addition to the passengers, there was a great deal of cargo being shipped on the *Titanic*. Which of the following was not part of the cargo?
   A. Tennis balls
   B. Ostrich plumes
   C. Dragon's blood
   D. Hairnets

7. The tickets for the *Titanic* varied widely. A third-class ticket cost about $35. A second-class ticket cost $65. A first-class ticket cost $430. A deluxe, two-parlor suite cost:
   A. $1,100.
   B. $2,200.
   C. $3,300.
   D. $5,500.

8. Some passengers brought pets on board. A woman named Marie Young brought prize:
   A. French roosters and hens.
   B. Ponies.
   C. Siamese fish.
   D. Racehorses.

9. How many bathtubs were there for the more than 700 passengers in third class?
   A. None
   B. Two
   C. 100
   D. 700

10. Which of the following was not found on the *Titanic*?
    A. Hospital
    B. Turkish steam bath
    C. Barbershops
    D. Ballrooms

11. The highest outdoor deck on the ship's stern was called the "poop deck" because:
    A. People who climbed up there were tired.
    B. Of a Greek word meaning "deck."
    C. Of a Latin word meaning "end of ship."
    D. That is where they walked the dogs.

12. Which of the following activities were **not** available for passengers on the *Titanic*?
    A. Miniature golf
    B. Swimming pool
    C. A photographic darkroom
    D. A mechanical camel

13. A passenger, Alfred Rush, celebrated his 16th birthday on the day that the *Titanic* sank by:
    A. Drinking champagne.
    B. Putting on long pants.
    C. Taking a Turkish bath.
    D. Smoking a cigar.

14. When the wireless operator of the *Californian*, a nearby ship, wired the *Titanic*, the operator is reported to have said:
    A. "We are in no danger."
    B. "Shut up!"
    C. "Our ship is unsinkable."
    D. "That is no concern of ours."

Name: _____ Date: _____

The *Titanic* (cont.)

15. Some of the passengers on the *Titanic* stated that it was possible to _____ the iceberg before they saw it.
    A. Smell
    B. Hear
    C. Taste
    D. Feel

16. Many experts feel that the ship might have been saved if the quartermaster who was at the wheel had:
    A. Done nothing.
    B. Stopped the engines.
    C. Put the engines in reverse.
    D. Turned quickly enough.

17. The *Titanic* was one of the first ships ever to use SOS, the new international signal for help. What do the letters SOS stand for?
    A. Save our souls
    B. Save our ship
    C. Send one ship
    D. Nothing

18. After all of the lifeboats were lowered and it was obvious that the ship was going to sink, those left onboard had several different reactions. Of the following activities, which is there no record of those left onboard doing?
    A. Reading a book
    B. Playing cards
    C. Riding an exercise bike
    D. Sending a telegraph to a newspaper

19. Which of the following phrases did not appear in the newspaper headlines on the day after the *Titanic* sank?
    A. *Titanic* Sinks, Many Dead
    B. All Saved From the *Titanic*
    C. *Titanic* Collision ... Being Towed
    D. Passengers Safe After Collision

20. After the *Titanic* sank, the talent agency that had hired a violinist who died in the tragedy presented the violinist's family with:
    A. A check for $1,000.
    B. A check for $10,000.
    C. A new violin.
    D. A bill for $3.50.

21. The men who survived the *Titanic* were:
    A. In demand to give speeches.
    B. Considered cowards.
    C. Offered jobs with the cruise line.
    D. Given lifetime passes on ships.

22. The *Titanic* sank because the iceberg:
    A. Punched a large hole in it.
    B. Ripped a long hole in it.
    C. Shattered a complete plate in the hull.
    D. Scraped off the rivets along the hull.

23. Who was Jason Jr.?
    A. The captain's son
    B. Mrs. Astor's pet Pekingese
    C. A remote-controlled robot
    D. A passenger

The *Titanic* Answers

1. **D. Maggie.** Margaret Tobin Brown from Denver was very wealthy. People know her today as the "Unsinkable Molly Brown." However, that nickname has been given to her only recently.

2. **D. Dining saloons.** The word *saloon* is taken from the French word *salon*, which means a large and fancy room.

3. **A. It was on fire.** As the *Titanic* left the dock in Southhampton, there was a fire burning in a coal bunker in the boiler room. The captain and crew weren't concerned because the fire was burning very slowly. Crew members were assigned to douse the fire with water, and after a few days, they were successful. The *Titanic* didn't collide with another ship as it was leaving, but it almost did. As the *Titanic* passed the *New York*, the *New York* came loose from her mooring ropes and swung out toward the *Titanic*. Quick action by the captain and the tugboats avoided the collision.

4. **D. Big enough to drive two trains through.** There were four oval-shaped funnels on the *Titanic*. The average height of the funnels was 63 feet. The average width was 19 feet, and the average length was $24\frac{1}{2}$ feet. The fourth funnel was a fake one, used to vent the engine room and main kitchen. It was added to make the ship look more impressive.

5. **D. 200 miles.**

6. **A. Tennis balls.** There were 76 cases of dragon's blood. Dragon's blood is not real blood but the sap of a palm tree found in the Canary Islands. It is used in the manufacture of make-up and to color wood varnish.

7. **C. $3,300.** Because of inflation, that would be the same as paying $55,000 today.

8. **A. French roosters and hens.**

9. **B. Two.**

10. **D. Ballrooms.** There was no ballroom on the *Titanic* because there was no organized dancing. There was a cooling room for passengers to relax in after they took a Turkish steam bath. There was a reading and writing room, smoking rooms, two barber shops, and a hospital.

11. **C. Of a Latin word meaning "end of ship."** The term *poop deck* can be traced back to a Latin origin *puppis,* which is Latin for the end part of a ship.

12. **A. Miniature golf.** There were many things for people to do to amuse themselves on the *Titanic*. Children could use a stationary bicycle or rowing machine in the gymnasium. They could also ride on a mechanical horse or camel. They could play shuffleboard, deck quoits, or games they had brought along themselves. Adults had other options. There was a swimming pool filled with seawater. They could play squash, take a Turkish bath, work out in the gym, play cards, read, write letters, or relax on the decks, in the lounge or in the smoking room. They could send messages to business associates or to friends on the wireless. They even had the option of taking still photographs and having them developed in the darkroom.

13. **B. Putting on long pants.** During this period, boys under 16 wore short pants.

14. **B. "Shut up!"**

The *Titanic* Answers (cont.)

15. **A. Smell.** Some passengers saw the iceberg, but strangely enough, some passengers, as well as crew members, claim to have smelled it before they saw it. Icebergs are from glaciers, and as they melt, the minerals in them give off an unusual odor.

16. **A. Done nothing.** When the iceberg was spotted and the lookout rang the warning bell three times and telephoned the bridge, the first officer went to the ship's telegraph and sent an order to the engine room that said "Stop! Full speed astern!" In other words, he wanted to stop the engines and then reverse them. He then immediately called to the quartermaster who was at the wheel and told him to turn. This was probably not the best strategy because a ship can turn faster if it is going forward. Had the engines not been shut off, the *Titanic* may have turned more quickly and avoided the iceberg altogether. Many experts feel that if the ship had not turned at all but hit the iceberg head-on, there would have been less damage. There might have been a hole punctured in the hull, but the hole would have been smaller, and the watertight compartments could have kept the ship afloat.

17. **D. Nothing.** It was chosen as a call for help or distress because it is easy to send and recognize as Morse Code.

18. **D. Sent a telegraph to a newspaper.** Many panicked, prayed, or tried to save themselves by throwing deck chairs and other items that could be used as rafts into the water. Some resigned themselves to the fact that they were going to die. One man and his brother went into the gym and began to ride on exercise bicycles. Several other men went into the smoking room and played cards. Another man, a journalist, went into the smoking room and read a book as the ship sank.

19. **A. *Titanic* Sinks, Many Dead.** The news of the *Titanic* sinking was sent from ship to ship until it finally arrived in America and Europe. Unfortunately, the messages contained few details and some inaccurate information. Some of the headlines from newspapers included: From the *New York Evening Sun,* April 15, 1912, "All Saved From *Titanic* After Collision ... Liner Being Towed to Halifax." From the *Daily Mail,* London, England, April 16, 1912, "*Titanic* sunk, No Lives Lost." From the *Christian Science Monitor,* April 15, 1912, "Passengers Safely Moved and Steamer *Titanic* Taken in Tow." Not until the evening of the day after the *Titanic* sank was the full story made public.

20. **D. A bill for $3.50.** Jock Hume, a violinist who died on the *Titanic*, was hired by the Black Talent Agency. After the *Titanic* sank, the agency sent Hume's family a bill for $3.50 to cover the cost of the uniform they had provided to Hume.

21. **B. Considered cowards.** Many felt that if a man had survived, he had obviously taken a spot in a lifeboat that should have been used by a child or a woman.

22. **D. Scraped off the rivets along the hull.** Until the wreck of the *Titanic* was discovered, most people thought that the iceberg ripped a long hole in the *Titanic*, causing the ship to sink. When the wreck was examined by Dr. Robert Ballard in 1985, he found that the iceberg had really scraped the hull and popped the rivets holding the metal plates of the hull together.

23. **C. A remote-controlled robot.** In 1985, a French/American team headed by Dr. Robert Ballard, an underwater geologist, examined the remains of the *Titanic*. It was on the ocean floor 12,460 feet deep. Jason Jr., or JJ as it was called, was a small remote-controlled robot used to take pictures of the *Titanic*.

Name: _____ Date: _____

Titanic Logic Problem

When we hear or read about the *Titanic*, we mainly hear about the passengers who lost their lives. In fact, some people survived the disaster and went on to live long and productive lives. Listed below are a number of actual survivors of the *Titanic* disaster. Also shown are the occupations of these survivors. Using the clues given and the chart on the next page, can you identify the first name, last name, and occupation of each *Titanic* survivor?

First names: Billy, Dorothy, Edmund, Eva, Frederick, Harold, Jack, R. Norris, Robert, Ruth
Last names: Becker, Carter, Fleet, Gibson, Hart, Hichen, McBride, Thayer, Navratil, Williams
Occupations: Architect, Actress, Banker, Businessman, Harbor Master, Magistrate, Night Watch-man, Salesman, Teacher, Tennis Champ

1. Ruth, Dorothy, and Edmund chose a profession that would ensure that they would never have to go near the ocean again.
2. The survivor who had the same name as the brother of a twentieth-century American president wore a suit to work every day.
3. Jack, a banker, once visited Becker's class.
4. When they worked, Fleet wore a uniform, Williams, who was a man, wore shorts, and Gibson wore clothing from different periods in history and different professions.
5. McBride, Carter, Fleet, and Hichens are all the same sex.
6. Neither Jack, R. Norris, nor Edmund are named Fleet.
7. Each month when Harold visits the company that Billy owns, he always makes a sale.
8. Whenever Dorothy or Ruth worked, they would appear before people.
9. Edmund Navratil once designed a theater where Dorothy worked.
10. You might expect someone named Fleet to be a harbor master, but he wasn't. Robert was the harbor master.
11. The first name of Becker or Hart was not Dorothy.
12. Hichen did not mind working on the ocean with boats every day.
13. As a class assignment, one of Ruth's students interviewed the magistrate, who was a woman.
14. The tennis player did not like his first name, so he used an initial.
15. Hart, the magistrate, and McBride, the salesman, got a loan at Thayer's bank.

First Name, Last Name, and Profession

1. _____
2. _____
3. _____
4. _____
5. _____

First Name, Last Name, and Profession

6. _____
7. _____
8. _____
9. _____
10. _____

Name: _____   Date: _____

Titanic Logic Problem (cont.)

Using the information on the previous page, solve the logic problem about the *Titanic*.

	Becker	Carter	Fleet	Gibson	Hart	Hichen	Thayer	McBride	Navratil	Williams	Actress	Architect	Banker	Businessman	Harbor Master	Magistrate	Night Watchman	Salesman	Teacher	Tennis Champ
Billy																				
Dorothy																				
Eva																				
Edmund																				
Frederick																				
Jack																				
Harold																				
R. Norris																				
Robert																				
Ruth																				
Actress																				
Architect																				
Banker																				
Businessman																				
Harbor Master																				
Magistrate																				
Night Watchman																				
Salesman																				
Teacher																				
Tennis Champ																				

Name: _____ Date: _____

World War I

Sometimes called "the Great War," World War I lasted from 1914 to 1918. It began with the assassination of the Austrian Archduke Franz Ferdinand in Sarajevo. Soon, all the great powers of Europe and eventually most countries of the world became engaged in the conflict. More than eight million soldiers died in the war.

Circle the letter of the answer(s) you believe correctly completes each statement.

1. During a battle in World War I, Cher Ami was awarded the Distinguished Service Cross for saving a battalion from artillery. Cher Ami was:
   A. A French schoolgirl.
   B. A nurse.
   C. A dog.
   D. A pigeon.

2. When American troops went overseas, they were issued steel helmets after they turned in their campaign hats, which were:
   A. Made into felt slippers.
   B. Given to new recruits.
   C. Made into bandages.
   D. Sold to finance the war.

3. During World War I, American soldiers were called "Doughboys":
   A. Because they were fat.
   B. Because they liked to eat pastries.
   C. After adobe bricks.
   D. After a French word meaning "tall."

4. Most of the heavy-duty weaponry used in World War I was manufactured in:
   A. The United States and Canada.
   B. France and Britain.
   C. Spain and Portugal.
   D. Italy and Greece.

5. In 1918 during World War I, most American soldiers were killed by:
   A. Enemy soldiers.
   B. Traffic accidents.
   C. Their own soldiers.
   D. The flu.

6. When Henry Ford, founder of the Ford Motor Company, learned that the army needed ambulances, he:
   A. Donated them to the army.
   B. Sold them at his cost.
   C. Sold them at full retail price.
   D. Refused to let the army have them.

7. Some people estimate that 90 percent of all the men fighting on the front line in World War I had:
   A. Cooties.
   B. Been wounded.
   C. Been gassed.
   D. Typhus.

8. Baron Manfred von Richthofen, a German who was the top pilot of World War I, is credited with shooting down 80 planes in less than 15 months. His nickname was the:
   A. Red Baron.
   B. Red Dragon.
   C. Red Devil.
   D. Red Knight.

Name: _____ Date: _____

World War I (cont.)

9. Germany's flying squadrons were known as:
   A. Luftwaffe.
   B. Flying circuses.
   C. Golden Eagles.
   D. The Black Knights.

10. Work clothing for American soldiers was called fatigues. What color were they?
   A. Olive
   B. Brown
   C. Blue
   D. Various shades of brown and black

11. Soldiers relied on horses and mules to move equipment and artillery during World War I. For protection, the animals wore:
   A. Heavy padding.
   B. Helmets.
   C. Gas masks and goggles.
   D. Combat boots.

12. When using the lightweight tank made in France by the Renault Company, the second man communicated with the driver by:
   A. Radio.
   B. Sign language.
   C. Kicking him in the head.
   D. Written messages.

13. In 1914 on Christmas Eve at the front, the German and British troops:
   A. Serenaded each other.
   B. Buried the dead.
   C. Decorated Christmas trees.
   D. Wished each other "Happy Christmas."

14. President Woodrow Wilson _____ to help the war effort.
   A. Kept sheep on the White House lawn
   B. Sold war bonds
   C. Joined the army
   D. Wrote a patriotic song

15. In 1914, much of the time at the front was spent:
   A. Racing and jumping.
   B. Playing baseball and boxing.
   C. Watching movies.
   D. Presenting plays and vaudeville shows.

16. Society women in London would stand on the corner and give _____ to young men who were not wearing uniforms
   A. Recruitment brochures
   B. White feathers
   C. Tickets to dances
   D. Passes to country clubs

17. Adolf Hitler, who was to become the leader of Nazi Germany many years later, received two Iron Crosses for bravery. He didn't mention these two honors because:
   A. He was too modest.
   B. He didn't know he had won them.
   C. He felt he deserved three.
   D. They were recommended by a Jew.

World War I Answers

1. **D. A pigeon.** Soldiers needed to communicate with headquarters from the front. Radios and telephones were used but were not always reliable. Telephone lines had to be laid from one trench to another. Poor connections, faulty equipment, and the enemy cutting the wires sometimes made communication difficult. Sometimes carrier pigeons were used to send messages. A message was written and tied onto the leg of the pigeon, and the pigeon was released. The pigeon would fly back to its nest at headquarters, and the message would be retrieved. Cher Ami, which means "dear friend," was a messenger pigeon that carried a message that saved a battalion from artillery. When the pigeon arrived, it had an eye and a leg missing. It was awarded the Distinguished Service Cross and was eventually stuffed and displayed in the Smithsonian Institution.

2. **A. Made into felt slippers.** They were cut up to make felt slippers for casualties.

3. **C. After adobe bricks.** The nickname for the British soldier was "Tommy." The nickname for the French was "Poilu." When the Americans arrived, they had no nickname. Several different nicknames were tried, such as "Sammy," after Uncle Sam. Although this name was used for a while, the Americans did not like it. Soon the newspaper correspondents decided to use the name "doughboy." The term doughboy probably came from the Spanish word for sun-dried brick, "adobe." Why was this name chosen? Cavalrymen began calling themselves "adobe" because they were covered from head to foot with dust as they marched. The term adobe was turned into the word doughboy.

4. **B. France and Britain.** The French built most of the artillery and the two-man tanks. Britain built most of the mortars and heavy tanks. No American-built planes were used in combat. A few observation planes were built in America.

5. **D. The flu.** In 1918, there was a worldwide influenza epidemic so bad that it even affected the war. It is generally considered the worst epidemic of modern times. It killed 20 million people worldwide and about 500,000 in the United States.

6. **C. Sold them at full price.** Most of the vehicles used by the volunteer ambulance service during World War I were made by the Ford Motor Company. They were not actually designed to be ambulances but were converted from the Model T. Henry Ford was a pacifist; in other words, he did not believe in war. Therefore, he charged full retail price for his vehicles. He did not provide a discount.

7. **A. Cooties.** The two problems the doughboys had to contend with were trench foot and lice. The soldiers were able to prevent trench foot if they would change their socks often when the weather was cold and wet. Most soldiers had lice, which were called "cooties." Not only were lice irritating—they would cause the soldiers to itch—they also transmitted diseases. In order to get rid of cooties, soldiers would routinely light a candle and run the seams of their uniforms over the candle to kill cootie eggs.

8. **He was known by all these names.** While most planes were camouflaged, Richthofen's plane was painted bright red.

9. **B. Flying circuses.**

10. **C. Blue.** Before World War I, work clothing was colored olive. There was a shortage of material and dye during the war. So the olive color, which is very drab color, could not be used in the fatigues; they were colored blue instead.

World War I Answers (cont.)

11. **C. Gas masks and goggles.** Since some of the warfare involved poisonous gases, it became apparent that the animals had to be fitted with gas masks just as humans did. While mules are not as affected by gas as much as humans, they still needed some type of protection. Their masks not only covered their mouths and noses, some of them included goggles as well.

12. **C. Kicking him in the head.** The motor was so loud in this tank that the only way the second man could communicate with the driver was by tapping or kicking him on the back of his head with his foot.

13. **All answers are correct.** There was little fighting going on, and everyone on both sides was sick of war and lonesome for home. The enemy lines were just hundreds of yards apart. The Germans shouted, "Happy Christmas." The French began to sing Christmas carols. When the British looked over to the German side, they saw decorated Christmas trees lit by candles being raised from the trenches and heard the Germans singing, "Silent Night" in German. First one side would sing a Christmas carol and would be applauded by their enemies, and then the other side would sing a carol and be applauded. The Germans and the Scottish Highlanders even played a football (soccer) game against each other. This lull in the fighting gave both sides an opportunity to bury the dead. At one funeral between the lines, the enemy soldiers from both sides gathered to pay their respects and to read Bible verses in English and German. When the generals heard of these events, they were furious.

14. **A. Kept sheep on the White House lawn.** He did this because of the manpower shortage during World War I. The sheep kept the lawn trimmed. The wool from the sheep was sold, and the money was sent to the Red Cross.

15. **All answers are correct.** World War I was a violent war fought fiercely by both sides. However, much of the time at the front in 1914 was not spent fighting but waiting to fight. When they were not fighting, the men had sporting events, such as racing, jumping, football, baseball, and boxing. They had film clubs that brought films to the front. They presented plays and vaudeville shows.

16. **B. White feathers.** In London, young men who were not wearing uniforms were given white feathers by society women. It was a sign of cowardice.

17. **D. They were recommended by a Jew.** Several years after World War I, Adolf Hitler was named Chancellor of Germany. In 1942, he gave the order to exterminate the Jews and to establish concentration camps, which were to be used for that purpose.

Name: _____ Date: _____

D **L** **R** **R** **O** **O** **F** **W**

D

E

M

M

U

O

S

C

T

R

W
E
E
F
H
A
T
S
R
E
C
D

Woodrow Wilson Quotation

Woodrow Wilson was the twenty-eighth president of the United States. For a time, he was successful in keeping the United States out of World War I by negotiating an agreement with Germany, which provided for the safety of passengers caught in submarine attacks. When Germany broke its pact and began all-out submarine warfare in 1917, Wilson asked Congress for a declaration of war. In doing so, he uttered a phrase that has become well-known when referring to World War I. Do you know what the phrase is? It is hidden in the frame around the picture of President Wilson shown above. To discover the quote, you must go around the frame twice, reading every *other* letter. Where do you start, and which way do you read around the frame? That's what you have to figure out.

Answer: _____

_____

B **A** **E** **C** **M** **Y** **A** **A**

Name: _____ Date: _____

WW I Logic Problem

A young boy was asked to return repaired army uniforms to soldiers in a hospital. When he entered the room, the soldiers were lying in bed talking. The young boy did not want to disturb them, so he listened and learned that each had a different military assignment, each was from a different state, and each had a different injury or medical problem. From their conversations, he was able to determine the home city, the assignment, and medical problem of each soldier.

He placed the uniforms next to the bed of the appropriate soldier and then left. How did he find out all of this information about the soldiers? Their conversations had a number of hidden clues. Here are the clues. Are you able to discover all the young man was able to discover?

Here are their military assignments: Armor, Artillery, Cavalry, Infantry, Pilot, and Sniper
Home cities: Denver, New Orleans, New York City, Miami, Minneapolis, and Seattle
Injury or medical problem: Frostbite, Wounded leg, Trench foot, Typhus, Gassed, and Blinded

Clues

1. The soldier from New York City with trench foot is in an odd-numbered bed and is not opposite the man from Seattle. The man from the cavalry is also not opposite the man from Seattle.
2. The soldier who was blinded is in a bed that is one number higher than the man who is in the artillery division and one number lower from the man from Miami.
3. The man from the armor division, who is not from Denver, has typhus and has a bed opposite the man who is in the infantry.
4. The soldier who was gassed is in Bed Five. Neither soldier on either side of him has a wounded leg.
5. The pilot from New Orleans is not next to the soldier from Denver or New York City.
6. The soldier in Bed Three is a sniper who is not from Minneapolis.
7. The cavalry officer is in an even-numbered bed .
8. The soldier in Bed Four looks forward to returning home, going out in his backyard, and picking an orange from his tree.

	1	**2**	**3**
Assignment	_____	_____	_____
Injury	_____	_____	_____
Home Town	_____	_____	_____

Aisle ═══════════════════════════════════

	6	**5**	**4**
Assignment	_____	_____	_____
Injury	_____	_____	_____
Home Town	_____	_____	_____

Name: _____   Date: _____

Vanity License Plates for Famous People

Vanity license plates for automobiles are popular today. A vanity plate is one an owner chooses that tells his name or something about him or her. While vanity plates are a recent development, what vanity plates do you think would be appropriate for some famous people in history? Given below are some suggestions. See if you can figure out for whom each plate might be the most appropriate. Some are quite difficult, so hints are given below. The hints are not in the correct order. Write your answer under each plate.

PL8O	SEZR	NYL QWN
1. _____	2. _____	3. _____

2TN KMN	2VNCHI	20WASH00
4. _____	5. _____	6. _____

IZBLA	BO NE	ToWELLn
7. _____	8. _____	9. _____

LIZ D QWN	ITLR	1ST KAN
10. _____	11. _____	12. _____

GR8 AL	ANT NET	JOAN
13. _____	14. _____	15. _____

1. A general and an American president
2. A Greek philosopher
3. A leader during World War II
4. A Mongol emperor
5. An English queen
6. A French emperor and general
7. A Spanish queen
8. An Egyptian queen
9. A duke who defeated Napoleon
10. An Italian artist and scientist
11. An Egyptian king
12. King of Macedonia
13. A French peasant girl who became a saint
14. The title of Roman emperors
15. Married to King Louis XVI

Name: ______________________________ Date: ____________________

U E C T A H N E T N F

U L O P Y O F E I P G D

F F E E E E D D A J H U U

D E E N R O D T N S U

Mother Teresa Quotation

Mother Teresa, who lived from 1910 to 1997, received the 1979 Nobel Peace Prize for her work helping the poor and dying. Much of her life was devoted to finding poor people who were dying on the streets in India and bringing them into a home, so they could die in peace and dignity. Her compassion also extended to children in the form of an orphanage that she established. Other women helped her cause, and a congregation of sisters called the Missionaries of Charity was established. The members of this organization, which is composed of sisters from many nationalities, serve the poor in many different countries.

When someone once asked Mother Teresa what one person could do to help the poor, she said something that is often repeated today. Do you know what the quote was? It is hidden in the frame around the picture of Mother Teresa shown above. To discover the quote, you must go around the frame twice, reading every *other* letter. Where do you start, and which way do you read around the frame? That's what you have to figure out.

Answer: ____

____

Name: _____ Date: _____

Sports

Circle the letter of the answer you believe correctly completes each statement.

1. During a 60-day marathon bicycle race, Bobby Walthour:
   A. Died twice.
   B. Ran over a judge.
   C. Was hit by three cars.
   D. Was struck by lightning twice.

2. In the 1850s, baseball umpires wore:
   A. Tuxedoes.
   B. Top hats.
   C. Disguises.
   D. White suits.

3. Margaret Waldron of Jacksonville, Florida, was legally blind and 74 years old when she:
   A. Rode across the U.S. on a horse.
   B. Ran a marathon.
   C. Hit two holes in one on a golf course.
   D. Swam the English Channel.

4. When Hessie Donahue met John L. Sullivan, the bare-knuckle world heavyweight boxing champion, she:
   A. Discovered they were married.
   B. Discovered they were brother and sister.
   C. Became his coach.
   D. Knocked him out.

5. In 1976, Dimitrion Yordanidis from Greece was the oldest person to ever compete in a marathon. He was:
   A. 68.
   B. 78.
   C. 88.
   D. 98.

6. During a game in 1919, Ray Caldwell, a pitcher for the Cleveland Indians, was:
   A. Arrested for assault.
   B. Struck by lightning but continued to play.
   C. Murdered by a fan.
   D. Married.

7. In the early days of softball, the game was known as:
   A. Softball.
   B. Ladies' choice.
   C. Lawn ball.
   D. Mush ball.

8. The game of softball was invented by:
   A. A Baptist minister.
   B. The Peoria Boys Club.
   C. Theodore Roosevelt.
   D. The Farragut Boat Club in Chicago.

9. The first water polo matches were held:
   A. In lakes.
   B. With horses.
   C. On croquet lawns.
   D. In Alaska.

Name: _____ Date: _____

Sports (cont.)

10. Table tennis was originally known as:
    A. Dining room tennis.
    B. Miniature tennis.
    C. Ping Pong.
    D. Paddle ball.

11. Table tennis was banned in the Soviet Union from about 1930 until 1950 because:
    A. They considered it a waste of time.
    B. It wasn't invented in the Soviet Union.
    C. They thought it hurt the eyes.
    D. It took too much time away from work.

12. During the Middle Ages, bishops imposed a ban on tennis because:
    A. It was considered an evil game.
    B. Too many monks were playing it.
    C. It was invented by a Protestant.
    D. People played instead of attending church.

13. In Paris, France, during the sixteenth century, there were more than:
    A. 2,000 fast food restaurants.
    B. 1,000 tennis courts.
    C. 800 swimming pools.
    D. 100 fencing schools.

14. In the middle of the nineteenth century, tennis was played in England on a court that was shaped in a:
    A. Circle.
    B. Square.
    C. Rectangle.
    D. Hourglass.

15. In 1938, boxer Henry Armstrong:
    A. Was knocked out by a nun.
    B. Was declared champion after he died.
    C. Was a famous chef.
    D. Held three weight division world titles.

16. Of which of his records was Babe Ruth, the famous baseball player, most proud?
    A. Pitching
    B. Home run
    C. Batting average
    D. Salary

17. Early rugby balls were made of:
    A. Pig bladders.
    B. Rubber.
    C. Jellyfish.
    D. Blubber.

18. Who was the first African-American to play baseball in the major leagues?
    A. Jackie Robinson
    B. Burleigh Grimes
    C. Fleet Walker
    D. Larry Doby

Sports Answers

1. **A. Died twice.** He was pronounced dead twice but recovered each time and finished the race.

2. **B. Top hats.**

3. **C. Hit two holes in one on a golf course.**

4. **D. Knocked him out.** John Lawrence Sullivan, the last bare-knuckle world heavyweight champion, was known as the Boston Strong Boy. He eventually lost his title in a bout to James J. Corbett. Jim Corbett fought for 18 years without receiving a black eye or a bloody nose. Here is how Sullivan came to be knocked out by a woman. At one time, Sullivan had a vaudeville act where he would ask who would like to fight him. Hessie Donahue, as part of his act, would come out of the audience and go on stage. She was dressed in bloomers and a loose blouse. She would put on gloves, and they would lightly spar with each other. The audience loved it. One night, however, Sullivan hit Hessie very hard in her face and she was furious. She quickly hit him back with a punch so hard she knocked him out. The audience cheered. The knockout was such a hit that it was left in as part of the act.

5. **D. 98.** In 1976, Greece's 98-year-old Dimitrion Yordanidis became the oldest man to compete in a marathon; he finished in 7:33.

6. **B. Struck by lightning but continued to play.** While pitching for the Yankees, the 6'2" pitcher was struck by lightning. The trainers revived him, and he finished the game, beating the Athletics 2-1. He was one of the veteran spitballers allowed to continue using the pitch after it was banned.

7. **D. Mush ball.**

8. **D. The Farragut Boat Club in Chicago.** In the 1930s, the game became popular throughout the U.S. because of two Midwestern sporting goods salesmen.

9. **C. On croquet lawns.**

10. **A. Dining room tennis.** The game began in the latter part of the nineteenth century. In the 1890s, Parker Brothers sold a version of the game they called "Indoor Tennis." It had small rackets and a light, firm ball with a knitted web that could be stretched across the dining room table. The net could also be stretched between chairs and played on the floor. The game was not very popular in the United States, but it caught on in England. An Englishman substituted a celluloid ball. In England, a version of the game was sold under the name of "Gossima" but everyone began calling it Ping Pong for the sound the ball made when it hit the paddle and then the table. The name was patented by Parker Brothers in the United States and also in England. It is the most popular racket sport in the world and the second largest participation sport in the world. Fishing is the largest participation sport.

11. **C. They thought it hurt the eyes.**

12. **B. Too many monks were playing it.** Tennis is similar to a game that was played by the ancient Greeks, Romans, Arabians, Persians, and Egyptians. It was played in monastic cloisters during the eleventh century. Many monks began spending more time playing the game than attending to their duties.

Sports Answers (cont.)

13. **B. 1,000 tennis courts.** Tennis has always been a popular sport, even though some rulers have attempted to ban the game. In the tenth century, King Louis IV thought the game was undignified and ordered that it no longer be permitted.

14. **D. Hourglass.** Major Walter Wingfield called the tennis game he introduced, "Sphairistike." It was played on an hourglass-shaped court with a net that was seven feet high.

15. **D. Held three weight division world titles.** Originally named Henry Jackson, "Hammerin' Hank" is the only professional boxer to have held three world titles at the same time. He won the featherweight title in October 1937. Then he won the welterweight title in May 1938 and the lightweight title in August 1938. He won 46 straight matches and fought until 1945. He retired with a career of 152 victories and 100 knockouts in 181 bouts.

16. **A. Pitching.** Many don't realize that before Babe Ruth set many records for his batting, he was an excellent pitcher. He was most proud of the fact that the first record he set was to pitch for $29\frac{2}{3}$ consecutive scoreless World Series innings in 1916. He did this when he was pitching for the Boston Red Sox. Ruth's many records have been reported, and some have been broken. One record, however, is little known. During the 1920 and 1927 seasons, Ruth hit more home runs than any **team** in the American League. It was during the 1927 season that he hit 60 home runs, setting the record of home runs for the season. His 60 home runs were 14% of all of the home runs in his league that year. Here's an interesting problem. If a player were to hit 14% of all of the home runs hit in a major league today, how many home runs would he have to hit?

17. **A. Pig bladders.** Today, basketballs and rugby balls are made from synthetic materials. Originally, pigs' bladders were used as rugby balls.

18. **C. Fleet Walker.** Moses Fleetwood Walker and his brother, Welday, both played for Toledo of the American Association in 1884. After that, Black players were barred from Major League teams. In 1947, Jackie Robinson broke Major League baseball's color line and played with the Brooklyn Dodgers. A few months later, Larry Doby was the first Black player in the American League. He joined the Cleveland Indians in July 1947, three months after Jackie Robinson entered the National League. Burleigh Grimes was a pitcher for the Brooklyn Dodgers. He was the last of 17 men who were permitted to legally pitch spitballs after the pitch was outlawed in 1920.

Name: _____ Date: _____

Mysteries From History

Read the following mysteries from history. On your own paper, write the solution to each mystery.

A Mesopotamian Mystery From History

The archaeologist made an exciting discovery in the area between the Tigris and Euphrates Rivers, which was once known as Mesopotamia. They discovered the remains of an ancient settlement of what was known as the Highland People. From past discoveries, they knew the Highland People were a primitive group of hunters and gatherers. They would follow the game and kill what they needed for food. They would also search for fruit, grain, and edible plants.

But this new settlement was different from those they had investigated previously. While there was evidence that the people in the settlement still hunted, there was also evidence that they planted crops and had begun to domesticate animals. By studying the tools of the settlement, the archaeologist believed that these people may have been the first in history to domesticate animals and to farm.

The archaeologist studied the settlement for several months and learned something that was very puzzling. The people lived in this settlement for only about seven years. Then, abruptly, they left. Why they left, the archaeologists did not know. There was no evidence of war or of an epidemic. There was no apparent reason for their departure.

A year later, the archaeologists discovered another settlement several miles away. As they studied this new settlement, there were several clues that these were the same people that had moved from the previous settlement. They raised the same animals and grew the same crops. but their tools were more sophisticated. This indicated to the archaeologists that the new settlement came after the first. But like the previous settlement, the people who inhabited this location only lived here for about seven years and then suddenly left. Why?

Over the next several years, the archaeologists found many other settlements of the Highland People. And in each, the people only lived in the location for approximately seven years before they packed up and left. Eventually, the Highland People settled along the rivers and did not move anymore. The settlements along the rivers grew until they became villages, and the villages eventually became large cities.

What baffled the archaeologists was why did the Highland People live in a settlement for only about seven years and then move? Once they studied the living habits of the people, however, they were able to understand why they moved after about seven years and then eventually settled by the river and didn't move. Can you figure it out?

Mystery From History—Roman Slaves

At one time in ancient Rome, it was suggested that slaves be required to wear special clothing so citizens could readily identify them and they would be easy to catch if they ran away. After a very brief discussion, the Senate decided not to pass this law. Why?

Name: _____ Date: _____

Mysteries From History (cont.)

Mystery From History—Swamp Warfare

The Romans moved into the fenlands of East Anglia after they defeated the British Queen Boudiccia. They had one problem, though; the land was very wet. As the Romans waded through the swamps, they were ambushed by their enemies. When they were waist-deep in water, they were vulnerable to the attacks. The Romans did not know what to do. They had never encountered this problem before. A new general arrived and devised a plan so the soldiers did not have to wade waist-deep in the water. What was his solution?

Mystery From History—Poisoning the King

As we read about the ancient kings in Egypt, the emperors of Rome, and the kings of England, it is fun to think about the power they had and how we might like to be a ruler with unlimited power. But no one's life during these periods was completely free of care. Certainly, the rulers and aristocrats had better lives than the peasants and slaves. But their lives were not completely carefree either. One problem rulers had to deal with was that other people, often relatives, wanted to kill them and take their place. In order to prevent this, a ruler might kill those he considered a threat.

Nero's half-brother Britannicus was worried about being poisoned, which was a popular way to kill someone, especially rulers. In order to protect himself, he had a food taster who would eat and drink a little bit of everything that Britannicus was going to eat. The idea was that if the food was poisoned, the food taster would die and not Britannicus. If the food taster did not die, then the person felt that he could eat and drink without fear of being poisoned. On one occasion, Britannicus had his food taster taste his food and drink some of his wine. Everything seemed fine. The taster did not become ill, nor did he die. Britannicus felt it was safe to eat and drink. However, the wine was too hot, and Britannicus ordered that it be cooled down immediately. When the cool drink was given back to Britannicus, he drank the wine and then died. Why did Britannicus die and the food taster did not?

Mystery From History—Roman Roads

A British archaeologist was excavating the ruins of a Roman rock quarry. When he found the road that all of the workers used to enter and exit the quarry, he studied it very carefully. Later that day when a fellow archaeologist asked him if he had learned anything, he said, "Yes, I have always wondered if the Romans drove on the left side of the road or on the right. Now I know. They definitely drove on the left." How did he know?

Mystery From History—Famous People

What did Socrates, Nero, Cleopatra, Marc Antony, Vincent van Gogh, and Adolf Hitler have in common?

Name: _____ Date: _____

Mysteries From History (cont.)

Mystery From History—Ancient Ireland
This Mystery From History is actually based on a Celtic legend. A legend is a story about a person, place, or event that is handed down from generation to generation. Sometimes a legend is based on some historical incident. This legend has many variations and probably is not true, but it makes a fascinating story.

In ancient Ireland, a king had two sons. Each son wanted to inherit the kingdom. The king decided that there should be a contest to determine his heir. Each son was put in a separate rowboat about one mile from shore and told to row in. The king said that the first to touch the shore would inherit the kingdom. The elder and stronger son rowed more quickly and was about to touch the shore when the younger son was some 20 yards behind him and farther out to sea. The younger son then had an idea. He did something that enabled him to win. What?

Mystery From History—Knights in Armor
Because knights wore armor, it was necessary for them to perform an action that has persisted to this day, even though no one wears armor. What is it?

Mystery From History—Buttons
Men's clothes have buttons on the right while women's have buttons on the left. Why?

Mystery From History—Boots
King George IV was King of England from 1820 until his death in 1830. He is not considered a great king, but he did start a new trend in footwear that continues to this day. His boots were different from everyone else's. The innovation concerning his boots was copied and is commonplace today, but at the time it was very unusual. What was it?

Mystery From History—Food for the French Army
One of the problems armies have always had was having an adequate supply of unspoiled food during their military campaigns. To solve this problem, a prize was offered by the French in 1795 for the invention of a method of keeping food safe for troops. Napoleon felt that a dependable source of food was important when he invaded Russia. Nicolas Appert, a chef in Paris, won the prize by inventing something that is still used today. What is it?

Mystery From History—Battlefield Collections
After many battles during the Civil War in the United States, some people would go onto the battlefield and collect something from the soldiers who had been killed. They would put these items in barrels and ship them back to England. What did they collect from the soldiers and why?

Mystery From History—New Doorways
During the eighteenth century, builders began redesigning doorways in castles and many buildings where the wealthy would go. Why?

Name: _____ Date: _____

Mysteries From History (cont.)

Mystery From History—Hundred Years' War

During the Hundred Years' War, whenever an English prisoner was captured, two or three of the fingers of his right hand would be cut off. But whenever a French prisoner was captured, his fingers would not be cut off. Why?

Mystery From History—Conquistadors

Whenever the Spanish Conquistadors were in South America, they sometimes had to travel through areas that were dense with foliage and unchartered. They often got lost. They learned that if they took a certain kind of horse with them when they traveled, they could always find their way home—even at night. How?

Mystery From History—Sailors

Bill Sanders was a sailor in the eighteenth century and led an exciting life. Bill sailed on sleek schooners and traveled all over the world delivering goods to exotic ports. Bill had one problem though. He loved rum. One day, his love of this alcoholic beverage got him into trouble. He and a shipmate drank rum all night, and when they got back onboard their ship, Bill was supposed to be on duty. Unfortunately for Bill, someone reported that he was drunk, and Bill faced the usual punishment—24 lashes. Bill told his buddy that he wasn't worried. He had been sentenced to lashes before but had never been punished. He said he had a secret weapon. On the day Bill was to be whipped, the first mate had Bill tied to the mast, raised the whip, and told a sailor to take off Bill's shirt. When the shirt came off, the first mate stood there with the whip in the air staring at Bill's back. Then he threw down the whip and shouted to the captain. "I can't do it sir. If you want it done, you'll have to do yourself, but I think it would be a mistake." What made the first mate change his mind?

Mystery From History—WW I Helmets

When World War I began, British soldiers were not provided with metal helmets; each wore a cloth cap. The number of deaths and wounds caused from head injuries caused the authorities in the War Office to be concerned, and they decided to issue metal helmets to each British soldier. They were convinced that this would drastically reduce the number of head injuries. The soldiers were happy with the decision and wore the helmets whenever they went into combat.

Some time later, the War Office decided to check the number of head injuries of their soldiers and compare them to the injuries they had before the helmets were in use. They were amazed to learn that instead of the number of head injuries *decreasing*, they had actually *increased*. The fighting hadn't increased. So why should the reported number of head injuries increase when men wore metal helmets rather than cloth caps?

Answers to Activities

A Greek Mystery from History in Code (page 37)
Question: What did the messenger see in the message?
Answer: At the end of the message was a notation that said, "Kill the messenger so that he can't betray us."

Roman Puzzle (page 50)
1. MISER
2. CEMENT
3. SERPENT
4. CAMPUS
5. BISECT
6. LIBRARIAN
7. INCH
8. INCENSE
Answer: REPUBLIC

Scrambled Headlines From the Ancient World (pages 62–63)
1. Antony and Cleopatra commit suicide after fleeing from Egypt
2. The Great Pyramid is erected in Egypt as a tomb of King Cheops
3. The Buddha, known as the enlightened one, searches for the truth
4. Julius Caesar is assassinated by Brutus to prevent him from becoming king
5. Hammurabi develops a code of laws in Babylon to protect the weak
6. A colossal Sphinx was built to protect a pharaoh's tomb from demons
7. Vesuvius erupts, buries Pompeii, no building remains
8. Hannibal crosses Alps on elephants to invade Italy
9. China builds Great Wall to protect itself from barbarians
10. Jesus Christ, whom many called the Messiah, is crucified for heresy
11. Olympic Games, a sports festival, is developed to honor the gods
12. Socrates, condemned to death, drinks hemlock
13. The alphabet, invented by the Phoenicians, is adopted by the Greeks
14. King Nebuchadnezzar creates hanging gardens for his beautiful wife
15 Egypt's greatest pharaoh, Ramses II, dies after ruling for 67 years
16. Hippocrates, the father of medicine, develops oath for doctors

Buddha Quotation (page 64)
Even death is not to be feared by one who has lived wisely.

Confucius Quotation (page 65)
A journey of a thousand miles begins with a single step.

Viking Puzzle (page 70)
sky, scare, axle, knife, odd, skin, wand, crawl, give, bait, raft
Answer: SCANDINAVIA

Runes (page 71)
<u>Odin</u> is not only a god of <u>war</u> and <u>death</u>, he is also the god of <u>wisdom</u> and <u>poetry</u>. It is written that he hung for nine days on the <u>world</u> <u>tree</u>, pierced by his <u>spear</u>. While there, he learned nine powerful <u>songs</u> and eighteen <u>runes</u>. His <u>throne</u> is in his hall in <u>Asgard</u>. From this throne, he can see everything that is happening in the nine <u>worlds</u>. He also lives in <u>Valhalla</u>, where the slain <u>warriors</u> are taken.

Medieval Fair Logic Problem (page 78)
1. Oscar, Barber, Red
2. William, Ale, Blue
3. Geoffrey, Sheep's Feet, Yellow
4. Sean, Thrushes, Green
Solution:
The first booth must be the barber. It doesn't sell the sheep's feet (Clue 4), the ale (Clue 6), or the thrushes (Clue 2); William is either in the first or second booth (Clue 4), but it is not the first (Clue 1); it is the second. Clue 4, reveals that the sheep's feet are in the third booth, and the green roof is on the fourth. The thrushes are not in the second booth (Clue 2); they are in the fourth, and the ale is in the second. The red roof, then, is on the first booth (Clue 6). The yellow roof is not second (Clue 3); it is third, and the blue roof is second. Sean is in the fourth booth (Clue 5). Oscar is not in the third booth (Clue 3); he is in the first, and Geoffrey is in the third.

Knights of the Crusades Logic Problem (page 83)
1. William, Beer, Bread
2. Geoffrey, Mead, Cake
3. Richard, Ale, Crackers
4. Cedric, Tea, Biscuits
Solution:
The knight who drank ale did not eat the bread or the biscuits (Clues 6 and 7). The knight who ate the cake also drank mead (Clue 1). So, the ale drinker must have eaten the crackers and, therefore, must have sat in seat 3 (Clue 2). Geoffrey must be in seat 2 or seat 4 (Clue 6). The knight who ate the bread must have had seat 1, since the tea was drunk by the person in seat 4 (Clue 4) The mead and cake must have been ordered by the knight in seat 2; therefore, the knight in seat 4 must have eaten the biscuits. By elimination, one must assume that

the beer must have been drunk by the knight in seat 1. Clue 3 reveals that Richard must have had seat 3. We know that Geoffrey had either seat 2 or seat 4 (Clue 6). However, clue 1 rules out seat 4, so Geoffrey must have had seat 2. Seat 4 was not occupied by William (Clue 4), so Cedric must have sat there. Therefore, William was the knight who sat in seat 1.

Family Coat of Arms Logic Problem (page 84)
Section 1: Red lion on a gold background
Section 2: Green oak leaf on a white background
Section 3: Silver cross on a gray background
Section 4: Pink rose on a blue background
Solution:

The oak leaf is green (Clue 1). One section has a red symbol on a gold background (Clue 2). The blue background is in the lower half of the design (Clue 5). The red symbol on a gold background cannot be in section four (Clue 2). It also cannot be in section two (Clue 1). It also cannot be in sections three or four (Clues 5 and 6). Therefore, the red symbol on a gold background must be in section one. The gray coloring must be in segment 3 and the pink in section 4 (Clue 6). One of the symbols in the bottom half of the design must be silver (Clue 4). If this was the rose, its background would be pink, and section 3 would contain a gray symbol on a blue background. But this is not possible (Clue 5). Therefore, the silver symbol must be the cross, and, from clue 6, its background must be gray. The rose, which must be on the blue background (Clue 5), must be pink (Clue 6), and by elimination, the background color of the green oak leaf must be white.

Scrambled Headlines From the Middle Ages and Beyond (pages 98–99)
1. French mobs attack Bastille, killing the Swiss Guards
2. William Shakespeare presents Hamlet at the Globe Theater
3. Joan of Arc, convicted of witchcraft, is burned at the stake
4. Johann Gutenberg develops movable type to print manuscripts more cheaply
5. Mohammed, founder of Islam, is born in Mecca on April 20th in 571
6. Christopher Columbus discovers a new world by sailing west
7. Magellan names the Pacific Ocean on a trip around the globe
8. Cornwallis surrenders at Yorktown to George Washington
9. Louis XVI and Marie Antoinette are beheaded for treason during French Revolution
10. Martin Luther attacks Catholic Church for selling pardons for sin
11. Duke of Wellington defeats Napoleon at Waterloo
12. Black Death, a devastating epidemic, kills 25 million
13. Crusaders enter Jerusalem and massacre Turks
14. Copernicus, a Polish astronomer, says sun is center of the universe
15. Pilgrims sailing on the *Mayflower* land in Plymouth
16. Kublai Khan, grandson of Genghis Khan, builds Peking

Titanic Logic Problem(pages 105–106)
1. Ruth Becker was a teacher.
2. Billy Carter was a businessman.
3. Eva Hart was a magistrate.
4. Edmund Navratil was an architect.
5. Jack Thayer was a banker.
6. R. Norris Williams was a tennis champ.
7. Frederick Fleet was a night watchman.
8. Robert Hichen was a harbor master.
9. Harold McBride was a salesman.
10. Dorothy Gibson was an actress.
Solution: This is an easy problem, and there are several ways it can be solved.

Woodrow Wilson Quotation (page 111)
The world must be made safe for democracy.

WW I Logic Problem (page 112)
1. Infantry, Trench foot, New York City
2. Artillery, Wounded leg, Seattle
3. Sniper, Blinded, Denver
4. Cavalry, Frostbite, Miami
5. Pilot, Gassed, New Orleans
6. Armor, Typhus, Minneapolis
Solution:

The soldier in Bed Three is a sniper (Clue 6). The man who was gassed is in Bed Five (Clue 4). The infantry soldier from New York with trench foot must be in Bed One, since he is in an odd-numbered bed, and he cannot be in Bed Three or Five (Clue 1). The soldier from the armor division who has typhus is in Bed Six, since he is opposite the soldier from infantry (Clue 3). Only three medical problems remain: frostbite, blinded, and wounded leg. Bed Four cannot have a wounded leg (Clue 4), nor can he be blinded (Clue 2). Therefore, Bed Four must have frostbite. This leaves two medical problems: blinded and wounded leg. The man who is blinded must be in Bed Three. (Clues 2 and 3). Therefore, Bed Two must have a wounded leg, Bed Two must be from the artillery (Clue 2), and Bed Four must be from the cavalry (Clue 7). This leaves Bed Five for the pilot from New Orleans (Clue 5).

Vanity License Plates for Famous People (page 113)

1. Plato
2. Caesar
3. Cleopatra (Nile Queen)
4. Tutankhamun
5. Leonardo da Vinci (Two Vinci)
6. George Washington (2,000 pounds is a ton, the word "Wash" in ton)
7. Queen Isabella
8. Napoleon Bonaparte (The word "bone" is apart)
9. Duke of Wellington ("Well" in the word "ton")
10. Queen Elizabeth
11. Adolf Hitler
12. Genghis Khan (Genghis was the first Khan)
13. Alexander the Great
14. Marie Antoinette ("ant" on "net")
15. Joan of Arc

Mother Teresa Quotation (page 114)

If you can't feed a hundred people, then feed just one.

A Mesopotamian Mystery From History (page 119)

After the Highland People had grown the same crops in the same location for about seven years, the soil became depleted of nutrients and was unable to produce a satisfactory crop. Since the Highland People were the first people to farm, they knew nothing about soil fertility. They just knew the land would no longer grow the food they wanted, so they left. Today, we know that by rotating crops and fertilizing lands, farmers are able to use the same land year after year and still get good yields. At this time, however, people did not understand this. So once the land became depleted of nutrients, they would move their entire village to a new location where crops had not been planted. Over time, they eventually located their villages and settlements along the Tigris and Euphrates Rivers. Here, the land could be farmed year after year because of the annual floods. Each spring, the floods would bring silt and sediment containing nutrients, and when the water receded, the nutrients would stay. So every year, the farmers had fresh soil in which to plant their crops. This is why they remained close to the rivers, and permanent villages and cities developed there.

Mystery From History—Roman Slaves (page 119)

It is estimated that one-third to one-fourth of the total population of Italy was made up of slaves. The senate quickly realized the special clothing would make it obvious that slaves outnumbered their masters in many places. They could easily overcome their masters and escape.

Slaves were sometimes criminals and sometimes prisoners of war. It is estimated that when Julius Caesar returned from his conquest in Gaul, he brought back 1,000,000 slaves. A slave was either branded or a collar was placed on him that said, "I have escaped. Send me back to my master." The number of slaves varied with the wealth of the slave owner. Some had just a few slaves, while wealthy people owned hundreds of slaves. Also, when a child was born of slave parents, he too was a slave. There was a famous writer named Pliny the Elder who owned 4,116 slaves.

Of course, emperors had the most slaves. Some had 20,000 slaves. With this vast number, each slave could be assigned a specific task. There were slaves whose only job was to polish drinking cups while others polished only eating utensils. There were food tasters, dirty dish-removers, and food servers. There were slaves that only took care of the emperor's city clothes, and other slaves that took care of his theater clothes. Some slaves that worked in the household often received money and sometimes even wages from their masters. When they had saved enough, they could buy their freedom. Some slaves were very enterprising. Occasionally, a slave would borrow money from his master and use it to buy a young boy who was also a slave. He would train the young boy and then sell the boy to his master for more than he borrowed.

Mystery From History—Swamp Warfare (page 120)

Stilts. The general showed Roman soldiers how to build and use stilts. At first this seemed like a good solution and worked well. Eventually, however, those attacking the Romans realized that if they could knock them off the stilts, they could stab the Romans while they were trying to recover.

Mystery From History—Poisoning the King (page 120)

In order to cool down the wine, cold water was added. The water was poisoned. By the way, in Asia there was a king named Mithradates of Pontus. He felt that one way to avoid being killed by poison was to become immune. So each day, he would eat a small dose of poison, and eventually, his body built up resistance to poison. When he was told that the Romans were advancing and that there was no hope, he tried to commit suicide by taking poison, but it didn't work because poison couldn't kill him. He had to kill himself with a sword instead.

Mystery From History—Roman Roads (page 120)

The archaeologist excavating a Roman quarry inspected the road leading to and from the quarry. He noticed the ruts on the left side of the road were much deeper than those on the right. Since the carts leaving the quarry would have been filled with stone, they would be heavier than the empty carts entering the quarry. The heavier carts would have cut deeper ruts into the road.

Therefore, he reasoned, the Romans drove on the left side of the road.

Mystery From History—Famous People (page 120)

They all committed suicide.

Mystery From History—Ancient Ireland (page 121)

The younger son took his sword and cut off his hand and threw it ashore. Since he had touched the shore before his brother, he was able to claim his father's kingdom. This story is told of the Kingdom of Ulster, and to this day a bloody red hand is used as a symbol of the province. As was mentioned before, this story has many variations. In some versions, the two vying for the kingdom are not brothers but rival chiefs. In other versions, they do not race on boats but on horseback, and the winner throws his severed hand across a river.

Mystery From History—Knights in Armor (page 121)

When knights in full armor passed the king, they would raise the visor on their helmet so the king could see them. This action in turn became the salute that military personnel still give to higher officers.

Mystery From History—Buttons (page 121)

Most people are right-handed and find it easier to fasten a button that is on the right through hole that is on the left. When buttons were first used, only the wealthy could afford clothes with buttons. Since wealthy ladies were often dressed by maidservants, the servant would face the lady; therefore, it was easier for a right-handed servant to fasten buttons that were on the lady's left.

Mystery From History—Boots (page 121)

He had a right boot and a left boot. Until that time, all shoes and boots were made to be worn on either foot.

Mystery From History—Food for the Army (page 121)

The canning process. Appert used bottles closed with cork and wire to win the prize in 1810. In England, at about the same time, the tin-coated metal can was patented. The Appert version and process for canned food is almost exactly as that used to this day. There was only one problem when the French army began using this new invention. No one had yet invented the can opener, so the soldiers used bayonets or knives; as a result, there were many injuries.

Mystery From History—Battlefield Collections (page 121)

They collected teeth from the dead soldiers. These would be made into dentures (false teeth) in England.

Before porcelain dentures were created in the mid-nineteenth century, dentures were commonly made with teeth pulled from the mouths of dead soldiers after a battle. The earliest record of a civilization making dentures was the Etruscans. The Etruscans lived in central Italy beginning about 1200 B.C. Throughout history, dentures have been made of stone, ivory, wood, and even animal teeth.

Mystery From History—New Doorways (page 121)

Hairstyles. Women had hairstyles that were so high that they would not fit through a normal-sized door.

Mystery From History—Hundred Years' War (page 122)

During the Hundred Years' War between France and England, English archers using their longbows posed a significant military threat to the French. At this time, the crossbow and the longbow were favored weapons. The French preferred the crossbow because it was accurate and sent an arrow strong enough to penetrate armor. The English preferred the longbow. While the longbow wasn't as accurate and the range slightly less than the crossbow, it could be fired faster. A good archer could fire ten arrows per minute with a longbow. The French declared that any English archer who was caught would have his index and second finger and sometimes even his third finger cut off so he would never shoot a bow again.

Mystery From History—Conquistadors (page 122)

A mare who has recently given birth to a foal is able to find its way to the foal. The Conquistadors knew this and would take a mare with them but would leave the foal at their base camp. Whenever they were ready to return to their base, the mare would invariably lead them back.

Mystery From History—Sailors (page 122)

It was common for sailors during this time period to have a crucifix tattooed on their backs so they would not receive a lashing.

Mystery From History—WW I Helmets (page 122)

The reason there were more head injuries with the helmets than without helmets was because there were fewer deaths. Before the helmets were in use, if the soldier had been hit on the head by a piece of shrapnel, it would have gone right through his cloth cap and probably killed him. After helmets were issued, it was more likely that a fragment of shrapnel would cause an *injury* rather than *death*. So, while the number of head injuries increased, the number of deaths decreased.